1972

# PATTERNS OF ACTION IN THE *AENEID*

# PATTERNS OF ACTION
# IN THE *AENEID*

## AN INTERPRETATION OF
## VERGIL'S EPIC SIMILES

By Roger A. Hornsby

UNIVERSITY OF IOWA PRESS    IOWA CITY

Library of Congress Catalog Card Number: 72–109594
University of Iowa Press, Iowa City 52240
© 1970 by The University of Iowa. All rights reserved.
Printed in the United States of America
ISBN: 87745–001–3

To J. L. H.

## Roger A. Hornsby

Mr. Hornsby earned the Ph.D. degree at Princeton University in 1952 in Classics. He has taught at The University of Iowa since 1954 where he is currently Professor and Chairman of the Department of Classics. He has been president of the Classical Association of the Middle West and South. He has published one previous book, *Reading Latin Poetry,* and numerous critical essays on Catullus, Horace, Vergil, and Plato.

# Preface

This book, an attempt to isolate and examine one aspect of Vergil's poetic technique in the *Aeneid*, is a result of pondering for several years with undergraduates and graduate students Rome's greatest epic. It has been written with such students in mind as well as for a wider audience of those interested in Latin poetry. The pleasure of writing the book has been touched with an agreeable frustration, for it never seems to be possible to analyze as fully as one would like any single passage of Vergil's poetry; each time one of his poems is read or examined more facets of its meaning and significance come to light. One could easily spend a lifetime on the *Aeneid* alone. Nevertheless, in this book I have tried to be as succinct and as clear as possible.

Any discussion of Vergil's poetry must depend in large part on the works of previous commentators, critics, and scholars. Indeed, of the writing of books on Vergil there is no end, and to keep abreast of the scholarly and critical publications on the works of Vergil threatens to become a full-time occupation. Fortunately, Professor Duckworth's surveys have lightened the burden.[1] Although I have tried to keep the documentation to a minimum lest it impede the line of argument and unduly expand the volume, it will be apparent to anyone reading this book how deeply I am indebted to earlier writers. Such men as Heinze, Pöschl, Knight, and Otis have afforded every student and reader of Vergil valuable insights into his poetry. In the following pages are cited the books and articles I have found particularly useful, and even when I have disagreed with some point I have discovered that the dis-

---

[1] G. E. Duckworth, "Recent Work on Vergil: A Bibliographical Survey 1940–1956," *The Classical World* LI (1958), and the sequel for 1957–1963 published in *The Classical World* LVII (1963–1964). See also K. Büchner's *Realencyclopädie der Classischen Altertumswissenschaft* article for further bibliographic help.

agreement has been fruitful for my own thinking. At the end of the volume is a bibliography which includes not only the works cited within the text but also useful works on Vergilian poetry as a whole.

It is a pleasure to record my thanks to Professor Rosalie Colie who encouraged the undertaking and who read and criticized the first draft; to Professor Erling Holtsmark who generously advised when it was needed most; to Miss Ruth Fiesel who sympathetically viewed the manuscript; to Mr. David Coffin whose painstaking care with the manuscript revealed both his friendly spirit and his devotion to Latin literature; to Mr. Charles Eisenhart and Mr. Patrick Mangan who substantially aided in the preparation of one draft of this work; to my helpful typists, Mrs. Donna Sandrock and Mrs. Eddie Baker. My greatest debt is to the person to whom this book is dedicated; to her rigorous scrutiny of both the style and the argument is owed whatever felicity of composition the book has; to her sympathetic patience and imagination is owed whatever success it has. Whatever blemishes or faults the book has remain with me.

# Contents

# Introduction:
# The Simile

The interpretation of the ancient poetry of Greece and Rome has undergone a profound change in the last twenty years. One need only think of such recent works as Steele Commager's *Odes of Horace*,[1] Kenneth Quinn's *The Catullan Revolution*,[2] or Cedric Whitman's *Homer and the Heroic Tradition*[3] to observe how deeply the once dominant historical and biographical approach to poetry has been modified by current literary criticism which investigates how poetry functions as poetry. In the light of the work done by such scholars it has become possible to see how complex the literature of Greece and Rome is, how carefully and purposefully it is organized. Among ancient poets who have profited from this renewed scrutiny has been Vergil.

Heinze's *Vergils Epische Technik*[4] laid the foundations of modern criticism of the *Aeneid*, but only recently have critics seriously explored its structural organization, its imagery and symbolism. One of the chief results of this critical activity has been the demonstration of how densely woven is the fabric of the epic. For example both Duckworth[5] and Knight[6] have shown us recurrent structural and metrical

---

[1] Steele Commager, *The Odes of Horace; A Critical Study* (New Haven: Yale University Press, 1962).

[2] Kenneth Quinn, *The Catullan Revolution* (Melbourne: Melbourne University Press, 1959).

[3] Cedric Whitman, *Homer and the Heroic Tradition* (Cambridge: Harvard University Press, 1958).

[4] Richard Heinze, *Vergils Epische Technik*, 4th ed. (Leipzig: B. G. Teubner, 1928).

[5] G. E. Duckworth, "The Architecture of the *Aeneid*," *American Journal of Philology*, LXXV (1954), 1–15; "The *Aeneid* as a Trilogy," *Transactions of the American Philological Association*, LXXXVIII (1957), 1–10; "Tripartite Structure in the *Aeneid*," *Vergilius*, VII (1961), 2–11; *Structural Patterns and Proportions in Vergil's Aeneid* (Ann Arbor: University of Michigan Press, 1962).

[6] W. F. J. Knight, *Accentual Symmetry in Vergil* (Oxford: B. Blackwell, 1939).

patterns throughout the *Aeneid*. Pöschl has indicated the importance of the storm scene of book I for the symbolism of the whole poem.[7] Francis Newton[8] and Bernard Knox[9] have persuasively argued that the recurrence of the imagery of the fire and serpent informs our understanding of the character of Aeneas, Dido, and the entire Trojan cause. Such criticism supports the notion that nothing is said or done or described at any point in the *Aeneid* without having connections throughout the poem. We have come to see that motifs, themes, and ideas are repeated in a variety of ways and in each repetition a new aspect of the motif, theme, or idea is illuminated. But further, each occurrence reflects on the previous ones so that we have a series of crosscurrents created in the work, which, when they are carefully observed, reveal not only how the *Aeneid* is organized but what it signifies. We are familiar enough with the idea as it applies to the successive appearances of various characters in the *Aeneid*, particularly Aeneas himself, so that it is possible to note that his character emerges as the poem advances until it attains its full stature in the final scene of the epic.[10] It is fair to say that as we finish the *Aeneid* we perceive that Aeneas' final act is connected with his first appearance and that the latter reflects the former as much as the first anticipated the latter. This same quality of reflection occurs in various episodes of the poem. To cite an obvious example: the motif of the hunt. In book I Aeneas goes hunting in Africa for food for his men, the first "action" he performs in the *Aeneid*. He finds and slays seven deer with which he feeds and refreshes his men after their harrowing escape from the storm (I. 184–194). His intention is clearly beneficent and so is the result. But in book II Aeneas and the Trojans hunt the Greeks, and in book IV Aeneas and Dido go on a hunt. In these two instances the hunting of Aeneas, profitable for a while, ultimately proves vain, for he does not achieve his goal, since each goal is for him a mistaken one: he was neither to save Troy nor marry Dido since in neither instance would he have "refreshed" his people. In book VII Ascanius also goes hunt-

---

[7] Viktor Pöschl, *Die Dichtkunst Virgils: Bild und Symbol in der Äneis* (Innsbruck: M. F. Rohrer, 1950). Trans. by Gerda Seligson as *The Art of Vergil: Image and Symbol in the Aeneid* (Ann Arbor: University of Michigan Press, 1962). The references to Pöschl are to the English translation.

[8] Francis Newton, "Recurrent Imagery in *Aeneid* IV," *T. A. P. A.*, LXXXVIII (1957), 31–43. (Hereafter referred to as "Newton.")

[9] B. M. W. Knox, "The Serpent and the Flame: The Imagery of the Second Book of the *Aeneid*," *A. J. Ph.*, LXXI (1950), 379–400. (Hereafter referred to as "Knox.")

[10] The development of Aeneas' character, his rebirth as a "civilized hero," Otis has well demonstrated. See Brooks Otis, *Virgil: A Study in Civilized Poetry* (Oxford: Clarendon Press, 1963), pp. 215–382, *passim*. The book is one of the most important works on Vergil. (Hereafter referred to as "Otis.")

ing, finds a deer and slays it, whereupon war breaks out; none of the Aeneadae is refreshed by Ascanius' hunt (VII. 493–510). Yet because of Ascanius' precipitation of war, peace and a new civilization will come to Latium. The dire immediate consequence of Ascanius' action ultimately results in good. The fact that Ascanius hunts at the opening of the Iliadic half of the poem just as Aeneas did at the beginning of the Odyssean half is intentional. Vergil invites his audience to compare the two actions, for they present an antinomy which is resolved in the final appearance of the hunting motif in book XII when Aeneas hunts and slays Turnus, whereby he is able to end the war and refresh the Trojan and Latin peoples.[11]

That episodes are repeated in subtle ways should need no further demonstration, nor should their capacity to reflect on one another.[12] The chief way in which the effectiveness of the technique appears is of course in the repetition of similar language. The recurrence of language invites us to recall the previous use of the same or similar terms, and when we observe that the same language appears in similar contexts it seems probable that we are justified in thinking that a pattern is developing. To cite an illustration: the verb *cupio* appears only nine times in the *Aeneid* and always in contexts of baneful desire. The more frequent word for "wish" or "willing" is *volo* (57 times). That the connotation of *cupio* in the *Aeneid* is baneful gathers confirmation from the contexts in which *cupido, Cupido,* and *cupidus* appear.[13] As their successive appearances demonstrate the passionate desire suggested by these words is a destructive force in the world of the *Aeneid,* and the implication of the pattern seems to be that such passion needs intelligent control if it is ever to be put to the advantage of men.

These illustrations of character, episode, and language indicate how interconnected are all parts of the poem. Begin anywhere in the *Aeneid* and reverberations of that passage in other contexts are discovered. Those reverberations will set off still others so that at last it becomes apparent that the *Aeneid* is a complex series of echoing and re-echoing patterns.

If what has so far been said about the patterned organization of the language, characters, and episodes of the *Aeneid* is true, it follows, then, that the similes of the poem should be part of this same rever-

---

[11] Note how throughout book XII Aeneas is described as hunting, tracking down Turnus, especially 466 to end. For a discussion of this motif see chapter 5, pp. 125 ff.

[12] But if further evidence is needed, see R. Hornsby, "The Armor of the Slain," *Philological Quarterly*, XLV (1966), 347–359. (Hereafter referred to as "Hornsby.")

[13] *cupido* appears 12 times, *Cupido* 3 times, *cupidus* 1 time. M. N. Wetmore, *Index Verborum Vergilianus* (Hildesheim: Georg Olms, 1961).

berating technique. And so I contend they are. How and in what ways the similes function and are interconnected is the burden of this book. Provisionally let it be said that the similes individually illuminate the various aspects and parts of the *Aeneid,* and through their repetition they define the patterns of action in the poem. In themselves, the similes form a pattern at the same time that they are part of larger patterns. But before we can examine Vergil's use of the simile, it would be well to consider what a simile is.

Superficially simile and metaphor appear to be varieties of the same thing, modes of comparison, as Aristotle remarked in his *Rhetoric* (III. 4. 1406b). Although both are linguistic phenomena, there is a difference between the two figures, a difference marked by the linguistic apparatus which distinguishes simile from metaphor, i.e., "like," or "as," or some such word or phrase. As a result of this linguistic apparatus, the words of a simile are used literally; those of a metaphor, figuratively.

To illustrate the difference between metaphor and simile, let us consider the two statements: "like doves the women fluttered about the altar" and "the women fluttered about the altar." The simile by keeping doves and women separate entities in the syntax of the sentence allows each word to retain its normal meaning and permits us to understand "flutter" in both its literal meaning and in a metaphorical one as well. The simile defines how the verb "flutter" is to be understood. In the metaphor, on the other hand, we are forced to extend the meaning of "flutter" without being given any specific directive of how to do so; we are obliged to infer that the women are like creatures which flap their wings without flying, perhaps like butterflies or possibly like birds. The metaphor leaves the choice up to the reader, and unless the context or something else clarifies the situation, ambiguity of meaning results. Metaphor and simile involve the comparison of two things of unlike nature which have a point of similarity between them, yet metaphor normally expresses only one of the two things and implies the point of similarity; it is, thus, a kind of brachylogy. Simile, unlike metaphor, expresses the non-identity of the two things as well as their point of similarity.

Simile and metaphor share another characteristic, namely a dependence on the gap between the two members of the comparison. To compare women to doves forces us to readjust our normal ways of thinking about women and doves in order to understand such statements. We ask how or in what ways such things can be compared, for we are aware that the two things are basically unlike. The unlikeness of the two things and the point of likeness creates a tension in the effect of the statement; the reader needs a kind of double vision to understand what is being presented to him. Much of the effectiveness of both metaphor and simile arises from this disparity and the need it creates for a double vision on the part of the reader. The poet can exploit at the same time both the similarity and the dissimilarity between the two things compared.

Metaphor, without complicating the grammatical construction of the sentence carrying the meaning, stretches the existing vocabulary of a language in order to say things that the language does not normally provide for. But the more a poet tries to specify by a simile the precise relationship between the two things the more diffuse and complex the syntax tends to become.[14] Following Stanford we can observe that simile is analytic, extensive, logical, and judicious; it aims at explicitness and definition. Metaphor is synthetic, intensive, intuitive, illogical and dogmatic; it implies more whereas simile expresses more.[15]

What has so far been said about the simile applies also to those similes of extended length and complexity which first appear in Homer and to which most critics have given the epithet "epic" or "Homeric." Metaphor and simile show their close connection only when the simile is extremely brief, involving only a word or a phrase. The ancient rhetorician Demetrius, feeling uneasy with Aristotle's discussion of simile and metaphor in the *Rhetoric,* appears to have been the first to note that the extended simile is a distinct literary device to which he would have denied the name simile, preferring instead "poetical image."[16] Demetrius seems to have been on the right track. Extended similes depend upon their length to achieve ends denied the simpler form, for in their extension they are able to comment on the object compared not only with greater scope and freedom, but with greater accuracy than does either the simple simile or the metaphor. Through the accumulation of detail "epic similes" become poetic images which explore and illuminate the object compared. The following passage illustrates this point. Androgeos coming upon Aeneas and his men is compared to a man who inadvertently steps upon a snake:

---

[14] On "metaphor" and "simile" see W. Nowottny, *The Language Poets Use* (London: Althone Press, 1962), pp. 49–71.

[15] W. B. Stanford, *Greek Metaphor: Studies in Theory and Practice* (Oxford: B. Blackwell, 1936), pp. 25–30.

[16] Stanford, p. 26, where he cites Demetrius, Περὶ Ἑρμην, 89.

obstipuit retroque pedem cum voce repressit.
improvisum aspris veluti qui sentibus anguem
pressit humi nitens trepidusque repente refugit
attollentem iras et caerula colla tumentem,
haud secus Androgeos visu tremefactus abibat.

(II.378–382)[17]

The simile defines the action of Androgeos and successfully conveys his feeling of horror. In addition, it suggests that the Trojans led by Aeneas are in some way like snakes.

Although I am sympathetic to Demetrius' term, "poetical image," I have retained the usual phrase, "epic simile" throughout this book, for the linguistic apparatus indicates that the long similes differ from the short only in degree. Furthermore, the following chapters consider both the short, brief simile as well as the long or "epic" simile, since frequently the one is as important as the other.

The simile, as has been noted, begins with Homer. It is part of the formulaic tradition from which the *Iliad* and *Odyssey* arise and often it is itself a formula.[18] But at the same time, as Lattimore has observed, it "is not decoration; it is dynamic invention."[19] One of the chief purposes of the simile in the Homeric epic is to "escape from the heroic";[20] it broadens the scope of the poem and juxtaposes, frequently, the scenes of everyday life and of common men with those of the heroic world of the epic. The simile in Homer, moreover, functions in a variety of ways, most of which, as we shall see, Vergil too employs. It can relieve the monotony of battle scenes, mark pauses or changes in the action, and end scenes.[21] The simile in Homer's epics illuminates a single, specific episode; it has, in short, single-significance.[22] But as Pöschl, Otis, and Knight have remarked, Vergil's similes go beyond such single significance. A given simile is "an integral—indeed a crucial—part of the motif structure" of an episode.[23] Vergil among epic

---

[17] All Latin quotations come from *P. Vergili Maronis Opera*, ed. F. A. Hirtzel (Oxford: Clarendon Press, 1900) and from *P. Vergili Maronis Opera*, ed. R. A. B. Mynors (Oxford: Clarendon Press, 1969).

[18] A. J. B. Wace, and F. H. Stubbings, *A Companion to Homer* (London: Macmillan and Co., 1962), p. 30. (Hereafter referred to as "Wace and Stubbings.")

[19] R. Lattimore, trans., *The Iliad of Homer* (Chicago: University of Chicago Press, 1951), p. 45. (Hereafter referred to as "Lattimore.")

[20] Lattimore, p. 43.

[21] Wace and Stubbings, pp. 70–71.

[22] Cf. Lattimore, pp. 43–44 and also A. Shewan, *Homeric Essays* (Oxford: B. Blackwell, 1935), pp. 217–228.

[23] Otis, p. 71, where he discusses the doe simile used of Dido in book IV. 68 ff. See also W. F. J. Knight, *Roman Vergil* (London: Faber and Faber, 1944), p. 171, and Pöschl, pp. 130–135.

poets may have been the first to achieve such integration. But I think the matter can be pressed even farther to show that the similes themselves are intricately interwoven and develop into patterns as well. The similes employing the same general theme, for example the storm, are all connected with one another.

But to return for a moment to Homer and his use of simile. There are in the *Iliad* 202 similes, 164 appear in battle scenes and 38 in other scenes. Furthermore, the *Iliad* has four times as many similes as the *Odyssey*.[24] Vergil's *Aeneid* has 116 similes, 46 of which appear in books I–VI, the Odyssean half of the poem, and 70 in books VII–XII, the Iliadic half. The proportion is in no way like that of the two Homeric epics. More interesting, however, is the fact that the books involving battles in the *Aeneid* (II, IX–XII) reveal that 50 similes are used in battle scenes or scenes of fighting;[25] that is, the similes are almost evenly divided between battle scenes and other scenes. These figures lend support to the notion that the similes are integrated into the fabric of the work in a way different from that of the *Iliad* and the *Odyssey* and serve functions other than simply relieving monotony or widening the scope of the work. Vergil obviously drew upon Homer's epics, but his intention was clearly different from his predecessor's. Not unaware of what Homer and Apollonius had accomplished, he set out to transform the epic and to accommodate it to his own day.[26] Among the changes he wrought was his use of the simile.

But now it is time to turn to the kinds of similes and the ways in which Vergil employs them in the *Aeneid*. Commentators have frequently noted that Vergil, like Homer, draws on the natural world for his similes: 85 of the 116 similes derive from nature; 31 of the 85 appear in the first six books; 12 concern animals and 19 the forces or phenomena of nature. In the last six books 23 of the 54 similes drawn from nature involve animals and the rest the forces of nature. The natural world and its denizens supply by far the greatest source of the *Aeneid's* similes, and almost twice as many of these appear in the last half of the epic. But there remain other sources than nature for the

---

[24] Wace and Stubbings, p. 70.

[25] The statistics are: II, 6 out of 11 similes; IX, 11 out of 12; X, 13 out of 14; XI, 6 out of 9; XII, 14 out of 17.

[26] See Heinze's entire work; also Otis, pp. 5–40; G. N. Knauer, *Die Aeneis und Homer* (Göttingen: Vandenhoeck und Ruprecht, 1964). A serious investigation of the simile in the *Iliad* and *Odyssey* is a desideratum. Though similes are repeated in varying ways in the Homeric epics, no consistent, intentional, pattern seems to emerge, nor do the similes seem to be arranged with the complexity Vergil employs. However, a thorough consideration of the simile might possibly reveal more patterns than has been so far detected or suspected.

poet to draw on for his comparisons: man-made objects such as jewels or statues; institutions such as cities; the divine world; or even the necessary rounds of daily life. In the *Aeneid,* 31 similes have their sources in such matters, 14 of them in books I–VI and 17 in books VII–XII. These statistics are not in themselves of great moment; it is only when the similes in their contexts and in their relationships with one another are examined that the significance of the simile and its recurrence become important.

As commentators and critics never tire of pointing out, Vergil frequently employs similes used by earlier Greek and Roman writers. Indeed, much of the comment on Vergilian style is concerned with how much he borrowed from this or that ancient author. An example is the first simile used of Dido in book I (498–503) which echoes the Homeric simile of Nausicaa in the *Odyssey* (VI. 102–109). Both the widowed queen and the nubile maiden are compared to the virgin goddess Artemis or Diana. But we do not need the knowledge of Homer's simile to see the point of comparing Dido to Diana, for Vergil's manipulation of the point of view as well as the details of the simile emphasize both the gulf separating Dido and the goddess and the disparity between the appearance and the reality of the queen.[27] Ancient poets, as is well-known, employ the motifs and traditions of earlier writers, but when the poets are as great as Vergil they do so in new and unique ways. The knowledge of Homer's or Apollonius Rhodius' use of the same material confirms the knowledge we can gain from the text. Although I am not primarily concerned with elucidating from whom Vergil borrowed his similes (enough articles, books, and commentaries already exist which explore this aspect of Vergilian poetry), yet one aspect of Vergil's borrowing is of some importance. It is an aspect which comes to light only through the accumulation of a series of similes drawing from the same general area of existence. The lion similes may serve as a case in point. Homer used lion similes in the *Iliad* to stress the prowess of Achilles, thereby suggesting his mightiness as a warrior. But in the *Aeneid* the similes are part of a different strategy. Although Vergil uses the notion of the lion to describe the strength of certain of his heroes, notably Turnus, the repetition of the simile in different contexts sheds a more complex light on the lion and finally on Turnus. We see the lion behaving in a variety of ways, all of which are appropriate to lions but not to men. The accumulation of the various views of the lion simile in the *Aeneid* fosters Vergil's con-

---

[27] For the discussion of this simile see pp. 89 ff.

ception of the hero as a man profoundly different from the Homeric hero. By repeatedly comparing Turnus to an animal, Vergil makes his audience fully aware of Turnus both as a mighty warrior and as a maddened beast. He thereby demonstrates how anachronistic is the conception of the Homeric champion in the civilized world Vergil portrays as coming to birth.[28]

The repeated use of similes with the same general motif has a cumulative effect. The poet may begin his series with a fairly detailed and complicated illustration and each subsequent simile recalls that first one and extrapolates its details and implications. For example, a wolf simile occurs in book II:

> sic animis iuvenum furor additus. inde, lupi ceu
> raptores *atra in nebula,* quos *improba* ventris
> exegit caecos *rabies* catulique relicti
> *faucibus* exspectant *siccis,* per tela, per hostis
> vadimus haud dubiam in mortem mediaeque tenemus
> urbis iter; *nox atra cava* circumvolat *umbra.*
>
> (II.355–360)

It compares Aeneas and his band of men to a pack of wolves who savage their enemies. I shall postpone the discussion of the details of the simile to a later chapter;[29] at the moment it is sufficient to note that the Trojans are likened to marauding wolves and in their behavior they ravage not only their enemies but also their own city.

The next occurrence of a simile involving a wolf is in book IX:

> ac veluti pleno *lupus* insidiatus ovili
> cum fremit ad caulas *ventos* perpessus et *imbris*
> *nocte super media;* tuti sub matribus agni
> balatum exercent, ille asper et *improbus* ira
> saevit in absentis; collecta fatigat edendi
> ex longo *rabies et siccae* sanguine *fauces:*
> haud aliter Rutulo muros et castra tuenti
> ignescunt irae, duris dolor ossibus ardet.
>
> (IX.59–66)

Turnus is described as a hungry wolf outside a sheepfold.[30] The simile recalls the earlier one used of Aeneas and his men as the italicized words indicate. Though not so complicated a simile as the earlier, it

---

[28] Otis, pp. 220 ff. and *passim* in chapters VI and VII.
[29] See pp. 63, 92.
[30] See also pp. 64 ff.

nonetheless employs similar details so that it achieves part of its effect from the repetition. One of the things, too, that the latter simile implies is that Turnus has assumed a role that once Aeneas himself had played. But by book IX Aeneas has become the educated hero. Therefore, by repeating a simile but using it this time of Turnus, Vergil allows his audience to measure the distance Aeneas has come in his education as a civilized hero and the distance which separates him from such heroes as Turnus. A further point may also be made about the recurrence of this wolf simile. Turnus is described as a wolf around a sheep pen, and the sheep are the Trojans beleaguered in their camp. If we reflect on the first wolf simile we can see that the Aeneadae were like sheep in wolves' clothing, for the greater part of Aeneas' band fall at the hands of their own townsmen who are unaware of the disguise. Vergil, through Aeneas who narrates book II, does not stress the point or even allude to it in the context of the wolf simile of book II, but the recurrence of the simile in book IX, where clearly the sheepfold represents the Trojan camp, implies that in book II the Aeneadae who attacked the Greeks like wolves were in reality only sheep. This discussion of the two wolf similes further illustrates a point which is connected with the reverberating technique of the *Aeneid*. The latter simile reflects light on the earlier one and affords the reader a kind of post illumination on the earlier.

The simile of the wolf is connected with the simile of the lion and, for that matter, with similes involving other animals. What connects them is the emphasis that Vergil places on the savage, wild behavior of these beasts. The similes, therefore, are connected not only within their own systems but also with other systems. The point can be illustrated by the wolf, the lion, and tiger similes of book IX. First, as we have already noted, Turnus is compared to a wolf threatening a sheepfold. The very next simile of the book (and the first lion simile of the *Aeneid*) compares the havoc Euryalus wreaks upon the Latins to the carnage of a marauding lion on a sheepfold:

> impastus ceu plena leo per ovilia turbans
> (suadet enim vesana fames) manditque trahitque
> molle pecus mutumque metu, fremit ore cruento:
> nec minor Euryali caedes; incensus et ipse
> perfurit ac multam in medio sine nomine plebem,
> Fadumque Herbesumque subit Rhoetumque Abarimque
> ignaros; Rhoetum vigilantem et cuncta videntem,
> sed magnum metuens se post cratera tegebat.
>
> (IX.339–346)

Note how this simile repeats motifs and language found in the previous wolf simile.[31]

Then at line 730 Turnus, after he is locked in the Trojan camp by Pandarus, is compared to a tiger within a sheepfold:

> ast alios secum includit recipitque ruentis,
> demens, qui Rutulum in medio non agmine regem
> viderit inrumpentem ultroque incluserit urbi,
> immanem veluti pecora inter inertia tigrim.
> (IX.727–730)

The fact that all three of these animal similes involve savage beasts attacking defenseless sheep clearly indicates their connection. But significantly, too, Turnus and Euryalus are likened: the Trojan and the Rutulian are comparable in their savage destruction.

Vergil then goes on to describe Turnus once more in a simile near the end of the book:

> acrius hoc Teucri clamore incumbere magno
> et glomerare manum, ceu saevum turba leonem
> cum telis premit infensis; at territus ille,
> asper, acerba tuens, retro redit et neque terga
> ira dare aut virtus patitur, nec tendere contra
> ille quidem hoc cupiens potis est per tela virosque.
> (IX.791–796)

He is likened to an attacked lion.[32] Because the lion simile is used of Turnus and of Euryalus, we are surely meant to see a connection, and the connection depends upon our recalling that Euryalus, the lion, was at last destroyed. To use the same simile of Turnus suggests, too, that he will be destroyed, and indeed as the lion similes progress throughout the poem we realize that the simile in book IX of Turnus as lion presages his own death. Again it is possible to see that the similes are connected and reflect on one another.

The accumulation of similes of the same sort and the relationships which obtain between the various groups of similes afford Vergil a means of revivifying what at first appear to be hackneyed motifs. To illustrate this point the bird similes of the *Aeneid* can be cited. They begin with a simple comparison of Hecuba and her daughters-in-law to doves in a storm, a not particularly exciting simile:

---

[31] See also pp. 65, 71, 120.
[32] See also pp. 68, 120.

hic Hecuba et natae nequiquam altaria circum,
praecipites atra ceu tempestate columbae,
condensae et divum amplexae simulacra sedebant.
(II.515–517)

But through the recurrence of nine similes describing birds in ominous
circumstances, and especially through two similes involving doves and
death, the first simile of Hecuba and the Trojan women as doves
attains a greater force than at first seemed possible.[33]

Without explicitly telling the reader what to think, Vergil, by
using the simile, can lead the reader to a moral judgment on an action.
To consider this point let us return to the serpent simile of Androgeos
to see how Vergil makes Aeneas condemn himself (II. 378–382).[34]
The simile depends for its effectiveness on its context in book II. Vergil intends his audience to recall that serpents have already played an
enormously crucial and destructive role in this book, for Aeneas has
just told his audience that it was by sea serpents that Laocoon was
destroyed, and because of his death the wooden horse was dragged into
the city where its concealed and fatal burden could begin the devastation of Troy. Through the narration of these events from the Trojan
point of view, Vergil indicates the close connections between serpents,
concealment, and destruction.[35] In the simile of Androgeos our attention is for the moment shifted from the Trojan Aeneas to the Greek
Androgeos; because of that shift we feel Androgeos' horrified surprise
at what Aeneas is doing. The appearance of Aeneas and his men has
been filtered through the awareness of Androgeos, so that Aeneas seems
like a serpent. It is as though Androgeos as representative of all the
Greeks who invaded Troy has been trapped by a device comparable to
that which the Greeks themselves used in entering Troy. But it cannot
be forgotten that Aeneas himself is narrating these events to Dido and
her court. In Aeneas' eyes Androgeos' reaction is a fitting one for the
Greek who came to devastate his city. But in the larger scheme of the
*Aeneid* the fact that Aeneas somewhat proudly narrates his exploit
ultimately tells against him and his men. They are, for the sensitive
reader, like the snakes in their deadly concealment and destructive
action. Although Aeneas does not think of himself as a serpent in any
serious way, he nevertheless unconsciously condemns himself in the

---

[33] See also pp. 24, 55.

[34] See p. 6 where the simile is quoted and also p. 61.

[35] Knox, essay cited in fn. 9 and also M. C. J. Putnam, *The Poetry of the Aeneid*
(Cambridge: Harvard University Press, 1965), pp. 3–63. (Hereafter referred to as
"Putnam.")

simile, for he shows his willingness to copy the destructive force of the Greeks, and so he lessens the nobility he thinks to achieve. By playing on the disparity between men and snakes, and by presenting the simile from the point of view of Androgeos, Vergil affords a moral comment on the Aeneadae and their action: he implies that the Trojans shared with the Greeks the responsibility of destroying Troy. The simile occurs at the start of a chain of events in which the Trojan band dons Greek armor and goes forth to battle. Eventually they meet their own men as well as the Greeks, but because of their disguise they are not recognized by their own people, and in the ensuing melee almost all of Aeneas' band are killed. The action subsequent to the simile of Androgeos confirms the implications of the simile: the Trojans like the Greeks help to destroy their own city.

Because of the poet's desire to specify the relationships which obtain between the members of the comparison, the epic simile provides an extremely useful instrument for exploring relationships and attitudes, and for allowing the reader to form judgments about a particular action or event.

Vergil not only uses his similes in the ways so far noted, but he also employs them as sources for subsequent metaphors. An example of a simile turning into a metaphor occurs in book II where Aeneas awakes after seeing in his sleep the ghost of Hector, and after mounting to the roof of his father's house beholds the attack on Troy:

> in segetem veluti cum flamma furentibus Austris
> incidit, aut rapidus montano flumine torrens
> sternit agros, sternit sata laeta boumque labores
> praecipitisque trahit silvas; stupet inscius alto
> accipiens sonitum saxi de vertice pastor.
> tum vero manifesta fides, Danaumque *patescunt*
> insidiae. iam Deiphobi dedit ampla *ruinam*
> *Volcano superante* domus, iam proximus *ardet*
> Vcalegon; Sigea igni freta lata *relucent.*
> *exoritur clamor*que virum *clangor*que tubarum.
> arma *amens capio; nec sat rationis* in armis,
> sed *glomerare* manum bello et *concurrere* in arcem
> cum sociis *ardent* animi; furor iraque mentem
> *praecipitat,* pulchrumque mori *succurrit* in armis.
>                                         (II.304–317)

Aeneas can only gaze like a startled shepherd at the attack on Troy.[36] The italicized words which describe the actual scene echo the motifs

---

[36] See pp. 15, 22, 24, 31, 36, 64, 91, 101.

of the simile: the laying open of the scene to view, the destruction by fire, the noise, the rush of all things in Troy being swept to ruin, including even Aeneas himself. The words retain their usual meanings, but because of the position of the simile at the beginning of the scene they have a metaphorical quality as well so that by the end of the passage the *furor* and *ira* have become the *flamma* and the *torrens,* they have become destructive forces of nature, impelling the awestruck Aeneas to plunge headlong to arms and death.

In another example of the same phenomenon, Vulcan, as he leaves the bed and bliss of Venus to go forge the arms for Aeneas, is compared to a housewife rising early to go about her household tasks:

> Inde ubi prima quies medio iam noctis abactae
> curriculo expulerat somnum, cum femina primum,
> cui tolerare colo vitam tenuique Minerva
> impositum, cinerem et sopitos suscitat ignis
> noctem addens operi, famulasque ad lumina longo
> exercet penso, castum ut servare cubile
> coniugis et possit parvos educere natos:
> haud secus ignipotens nec tempore segnior illo
> mollibus e stratis opera ad fabrilia surgit.    (407–415)

> . . . . . . . . . . . . . . . .

> hoc tunc ignipotens caelo *descendit* ab alto.    (423)

> . . . . . . . . . . . . . . . .

> '*tollite cuncta*' inquit '*coeptosque auferte labores,*
> *Aetnaei Cyclopes, et huc advertite mentem:*
> *arma acri facienda viro. nunc viribus usus,*
> *nunc manibus rapidis, omni nunc arte magistra.*
> *praecipitate moras.*' nec plura effatus, at illi
> ocius *incubuere* omnes pariterque *laborem*
> *sortiti.* . . .                           (439–445)
> (VIII.407–445, *passim*)

When Vulcan arrives at his smithy and directs the Cyclopes in their tasks, the language used applies both to what he is doing and to the housewife of the simile as well. The italicized words, especially his address to the Cyclopes, indicate how the themes of the simile are worked out: the Cyclopes are treated as the servants are in the simile; the need for efficiency and speed in both cases; the housewife's concern for her husband and children is echoed in Vulcan's concern for Aeneas; and over-all the directing intelligence of the housewife on the one hand and the god on the other. The words of the passage acquire a metaphorical significance because of the simile which precedes the description of Vulcan's behavior.[37]

A converse process can also occur when the simile appears at the end of a passage of description. In the following example the Trojans return to battle after being heartened by the sudden appearance of Apollo who granted Ascanius' prayer to be allowed to kill one of the enemy:

> ergo avidum pugnae dictis ac numine Phoebi
> Ascanium prohibent, ipsi in certamina rursus
> *succedunt* animasque in *aperta* pericula *mittunt.*
> *it clamor* totis per propugnacula muris,
> *intendunt acris arcus amentaque torquent.*
> *sternitur* omne solum telis, tum scuta *cavae*que
> *dant sonitum flictu galeae,* pugna *aspera surgit:*
> quantus ab occasu veniens pluvialibus Haedis
> verberat imber humum, quam multa grandine nimbi
> in vada praecipitant, cum Iuppiter horridus Austris
> torquet aquosam hiemem et caelo cava nubila rumpit.
>
> (IX.661–671)

From the italicized words it can be seen how the simile picks up the language of the preceding passage: the movement into battle, the noise, the use of weapons to destroy, and the surge of fighting find their counterpart in the wintry storm of the simile.[38] In reading the simile we feel its rightness or fitness, for its language recapitulates the themes already adumbrated in the preceding narrative. But furthermore the simile reflects upon the passage itself so that the words italicized, which initially carried only their normal meaning, acquire in the light of the simile a metaphorical significance.

Analogous to these processes is another wherein a simile or system of similes finds the origin of its power in a scene or a simple narration which may well be far prior to the appearance of the simile. No greater example of this occurs in the *Aeneid* than the storm similes. As we will see in chapter one, the first storm simile occurs in book II (304–308), but the source for this simile and the entire system of storm similes is the great storm which opens the action of the *Aeneid*. All the subsequent similes echo the violence and powerfulness of the storm which blew Aeneas off course and into an African harbor.

---

[37] See also pp. 105, 106.
[38] See also pp. 33, 40.

Pöschl properly pointed out that the storm described at the opening of the *Aeneid* is a powerful symbol of the conflicts which rage within the course of the poem.[39] But it becomes a symbol only in the light of what happens subsequently and the language used to describe those events. Had Vergil not employed the storm as a source for some of his ensuing similes and used it also as a parallel for subsequent action, the storm by itself would not have attained its symbolic function. It is significant that the winds which blow upon the fleet of Aeneas are first compared to a line of march: *ac venti velut agmine facto* (I. 82), for, by the end of the *Aeneid*, in book XII, the terms are reversed, the whirlwind is used for the action of the Trojans, especially of Aeneas. The battle-field of the Latins and Trojans has become the sea surging under the storm of battle. How Vergil works all these matters out will become apparent when the entire system of the storm similes is examined in chapter one.[40] For the moment, let it be enough to remark that the storm of book I heralds not only the storm of passion which engulfs Dido and almost destroys Aeneas but also the storm of battle which more importantly threatens to destroy Aeneas and his mission, the establishing of a civilization in Latium.

The similes of the *Aeneid* afford us one way of approaching and understanding both the poem and Vergilian poetic practice. Through them we can apprehend something of what the poet is attempting to achieve as well as how he achieves it. The following chapters explore the similes of the *Aeneid* and what they reveal about the poem and its effectiveness as one of the great works of western European literature. Although each simile is located in its particular context, I have not felt it necessary to comment on the organization of any particular book nor on the *Aeneid* as a whole; enough adequate works on the structural organization of the *Aeneid* are now available.[41] Further, I have been concerned with the similes of the *Aeneid* alone, not with those which appear in the rest of the Vergilian corpus, for this would involve the problem of Vergil's development as an artist, a topic I shall leave for a later work. Finally, a *caveat* should be voiced. The similes are but one part of the *Aeneid,* and while they afford a way into the work, they do not function apart from all the other elements which Vergil uses: the metaphors, the plot, the organization of the episodes, the development of the characters, the structure of the entire poem.

---

[39] Pöschl, pp. 24–33.
[40] See also chapter 7 on the storm imagery of book XII, especially pp. 123 ff.
[41] See especially Otis' work and the essays and book by Duckworth, cited in fn. 5.

The first three chapters discuss the similes which draw from the world of nature. The fourth considers those which surround the three chief characters of the *Aeneid,* Dido and Turnus in relation to Aeneas. The next two chapters concern the similes based upon the gods and the world of men, both of which topics have connections with the imiles used of the chief actors in the poem. The final chapter explores the similes of book XII. In chapters 1, 2, 3, 5, 6, the similes are arranged on the basis of common subject matter and then on the order of their appearance in the *Aeneid*; whereas in two chapters, 4 and 7, the arrangement is based solely on order of appearance. Necessarily, a certain amount of cross-reference occurs, especially when one complex simile has several parts to it and each part deserves individual comment. I have tried to keep such occasions to a minimum, but I have indicated in the footnotes where the relevant discussions appear. Any scheme of presenting the similes of the *Aeneid* could involve a rigidity that would obscure more than illuminate, therefore I have not felt compelled to be inflexible in the arrangement of the similes for discussion. Furthermore, by the arrangement chosen, I hope it will be apparent by the end of the book that Vergil's use of similes functions in a variety of ways to illuminate not only the similes themselves in their cross-connections but also the characters of the poem and their interrelationships, and finally the organization and theme of the *Aeneid* as a whole.[42]

---

[42] I should also make it clear that not every passage capable of being construed as a simile will be discussed. Those involving one or two words, such as that at V. 254 or at V. 317 are little more than periphrases. Long, epic similes are the basis for the book and the short ones are used only for illumination of them. One hundred and sixteen similes are discussed in the text.

*Chapter 1*

# The World of Nature:
# The Elements

The havoc men wreak in war is like the unleashed fury of a raging storm or a wind-tossed sea or a rampaging river which devastate all they encounter. In the similes of the *Aeneid* the gale of the winds occurs either as the harbinger of storms or as their proximate cause; the fury of the winds unleashes the fury of the sea or river or increases the force of rain or hail. Vergil uses these similes of violent nature, emphasizing now one aspect and now another, in order to illuminate men's behavior. An examination of the storm similes reveals a deliberate pattern in their appearance, a pattern which reflects particularly on the change and development of Aeneas and the Trojan cause.

All such similes, furthermore, derive their power not only from their particular context but also from the storm scene which opens the action of the *Aeneid*. The storm in book I is not a simile but an event in the history of the Trojans. But by the accumulation of similes deliberately designed to recall the storm, that violent eruption of nature becomes as Pöschl observed[1] a symbolic event foreshadowing much of the action of the *Aeneid*. Characteristically Vergil's reverberating technique allows the first event of the *Aeneid* to attain its full significance only at the end of the poem.

Although the storm scene itself need not be reviewed here, the similes framing that scene deserve comment, for they both illuminate the scene itself and play a part in preparing for the subsequent similes

---

[1] Pöschl, chapter I, "Basic Themes," but especially pp. 24–33.

of violent nature and their significance. The first occurs within the first hundred lines:

> Haec ubi dicta, cavum conversa cuspide montem
> impulit in latus; ac venti velut agmine facto,
> qua data porta, ruunt et terras turbine perflant.
>
> (I.81–83)

In acceding to Juno's request, Aeolus releases the winds, which are here described in a phrase heavy with military connotation, *agmine facto*. This connotation is reinforced by the ambiguous phrase of the next line, *qua data porta,* which implies the gate of a fortified city suddenly forced by the onrush of men. The important point about the simile lies in the comparison of a natural phenomenon to a human activity. The comparison is made, however, in a deliberately restrained fashion. Though this is the first simile to appear in the *Aeneid,* Vergil elects not to employ a full-scale epic simile, preferring instead to understate his point. By hinting in the simile at the personification of the winds, a rhetorical device Vergil will use to describe the attack of the storm on Aeneas and his men, Vergil emphasizes the disparity which exists between men and winds, for the winds are, as the language denotes, merely motion, merely a force undirected by a controlling intelligence. Indeed, as the storm develops, it is clear that the winds are not themselves consciously aiming to destroy Aeneas; he is the chance victim of their undirected turbulence.[2]

This understated simile effectively heralds the storm and prepares the way for the long epic simile which concludes the passage:

> ac veluti magno in populo cum saepe coorta est
> seditio saevitque animis ignobile vulgus
> iamque faces et saxa volant, furor arma ministrat;
> tum, pietate gravem ac meritis si forte virum quem
> conspexere, silent arrectisque auribus astant;
> ille regit dictis animos et pectora mulcet:
> sic cunctus pelagi cecidit fragor, aequora postquam
> prospiciens genitor caeloque invectus aperto
> flectit equos curruque volans dat lora secundo.
>
> (I.148–156)

---

[2] That Juno is the ultimate cause of the storm in no way invalidates the argument. Her removal of herself from the actual deed is typical of her behavior throughout the *Aeneid*. Her refusal to take the responsibility for directing what she wants reduces the effectiveness of her plans and forces her to compromise. For a discussion of the releasing of the winds as an analogue for the releasing of madness, see Putnam, pp. 8–16.

The simile, one of the most famous in the *Aeneid*,[3] compares Neptune, who has just asserted his rule over the sea and forced the winds to retreat, to the statesman who by his serious, responsible manner can calm the spirit of a mob threatening destruction. As others have noted, comparing the storm to a political reality is one of Vergil's great achievements, but there is even more to be observed about the simile. First of all, a god is compared to a man. The simile marks the moral advance from chaos to order, for Neptune has become the controlling intelligence directing the wilful winds; unlike Juno, but like the statesman of the simile, he assumes responsibility for his action.

Next, the two framing similes are of the utmost importance in understanding the *Aeneid* as a whole and also the thought underlying many subsequent similes involving men and elemental forces. The first two similes compare the violence of nature to that of men, but in subsequent similes the terms are reversed—the violence of men is likened to that of nature. At the very outset of his poem Vergil establishes a similarity between the violence of nature and of men. But by using as his first term in these similes the mindless violence of nature and then by reversing the terms he brings to the fore the notion of the mindlessness of men's violence. But men are not mindless nor are they to be held irresponsible for their actions. Hence the second framing simile: that of a divine or human controlling intelligence, directing and ordering the human or elemental forces. The radical distinction between men and nature lies at the heart of many of the man-nature similes; it allows Vergil to suggest the moral irresponsibility of much men do and opens the way for moral judgment upon their actions. The Neptune-as-wise-statesman simile embodies the ideal of human conduct and foreshadows what Aeneas himself will become, as the use of *pietate* (151) hints, just as the "Romanness" of the scene (cf. *magno in populo*) suggests the ultimate Roman order.[4]

After the framing similes of the storm scene, the first simile to involve the violent eruption of nature appears in book II. Aeneas tells Dido and her court that after his encounter in his sleep with the ghost of Hector he awoke to find Troy invaded by the Greeks. Climbing to the roof of his father's house, he looks out upon the scene of devastation which he describes as follows:

---

[3] For observations about the relationship of the simile to politics see Pöschl, p. 23; for its relationship to the motifs of *furor-pietas*, see Otis, pp. 229–230; for an analysis see L. A. Constans, *L'Énéide de Virgile* (Paris: Mallotie, 1938), pp. 50–51.

[4] See Otis, pp. 229–230.

> in segetem veluti cum flamma furentibus Austris
> incidit, aut rapidus montano flumine torrens
> sternit agros, sternit sata laeta boumque labores
> praecipitisque trahit silvas; stupet inscius alto
> accipiens sonitum saxi de vertice pastor.
>
> (II.304–308)

The Greek forces are comparable to such natural forces as a blaze fanned by the south wind, or the torrent of a mountain stream, which destroy fields, farms, and forests.[5] Aeneas compares himself to an amazed and powerless shepherd who watches the destruction from a height. The simile makes clear that so far as Aeneas is concerned the invasion of the Greeks was as unexpected and as irresistible as the storm in book I had been. It is worth noting that the south wind is the proximate cause for fanning the fire, just as the winds had been the cause earlier for the stirring up of the seas. The use of *inscius*[6] implies an uncomprehending wonder which can take in neither the full extent of the attack nor the reason for it, even as one cannot understand or fathom the causes for natural disasters but only endure them. This sense of bewilderment in the simile reinforces our awareness that the effect of what Aeneas witnesses is like the effect of the storm, for Aeneas, warned by Hector to flee, is deflected from leaving Troy, just as he was deflected from Italy by the incomprehensible storm which beset him and drove him to Africa. In employing as equivalences fire and water, the simile shows the power of the two elements for harm; at this point no discrimination between them is made, but in the course of their recurrence in the *Aeneid* a discrimination between them will appear.

The next simile of violence in nature shows even more clearly its dependence upon the storm of book I:

> adversi rupto ceu quondam turbine venti
> confligunt, Zephyrusque Notusque et laetus Eois
> Eurus equis; stridunt silvae saevitque tridenti
> spumeus atque imo Nereus ciet aequora fundo.
>
> (II.416–419)

Aeneas and his men disguised as Greeks, and a party of Greeks with the recently captured Cassandra, have engaged in deadly combat.

---

[5] See also p. 13 and pp. 31, 64, 91, 101.

[6] On the use of *inscius* and *nescius* in the *Aeneid* see, R. A. Hornsby, "The *Pastor* in the Poetry of Vergil," *Classical Journal*, LXIII (1968), 148, fn. 6, where the distinctions Vergil observes in the two words are discussed.

Greek reinforcements arrive from all sides, *acerrimus Ajax / et gemini Atridae Dolopumque exercitus omnis* (414–415). These men are compared to the battling winds, which are personified as Zephyrus, Notus, and Eurus, the same personification which occurred in the storm scene of book I. Furthermore, the details of the trees shrieking and of Nereus with his trident calling up the depths of the sea vividly recall the storm of book I with its loud crashes and stirred-up sea.

The simile marks the turning point in the fortunes of Aeneas and his men at Troy. He and his band, disguised as Greeks, have been successful in attacking their enemy, but with the arrival of the Greeks that very disguise calls down havoc on its wearers. The fact that Aeneas narrates the events of book II and so is to be regarded as creating the simile implies that Aeneas himself perceives a connection between the attacking Greeks and the storm at sea. For significantly in the simile Nereus possesses the trident and calls up the threatening sea, unlike Neptune of book I who with his trident calms the sea. Nereus, a minor deity, lacks the power and moral force to rule the winds. No statesman is here, for the gods, as Aeneas subsequently discovers, have condemned Troy. The Greeks are to vent their fury even as the winds, and only their own exhaustion can bring an end to destruction.

To the reader of the *Aeneid,* the fact that Nereus in the simile stirs up the storm and not Neptune reinforces the notion, suggested in book I, that the natural world, as represented by the storm calmed by Neptune, will no longer be hostile to Aeneas and his men. But Aeneas in narrating his past cannot know that nature will in the future be clement. He sees the similarity between the brawling men and brawling nature, and so he indicates his awareness of the hostility that exists between the Trojans and the world around them. Through such a detail Vergil does not allow his hero to perceive as fully as he expects the reader to. The complexity of the position of the simile, as well as the simile itself, reflects both Aeneas' point of view and Vergil's attitude towards it. In employing the simile, Aeneas shows his awareness of the isolation in which he and his men exist; Vergil, by presenting his hero's perspective, implies that Aeneas must be further educated before he can appreciate the full import of both his words and experiences. Thus for Vergil's audience not only the simile with its reverberations but also the hysteron-proteron arrangement of books I, II, and III afford a deeper insight than Aeneas'. For we now can see that the storm scene of book I was like the storm of the Greeks sacking Troy, and we can now understand that in the figure of Neptune, who calmed the winds and sea, the divine and natural worlds have changed: the remnant of Trojans will no longer suffer in an utterly alien and hostile world. By showing us what things had been like, Vergil is able to indicate what improvement has been made and to adumbrate the future.

The Greeks again appear in book II in a simile comparable to the previous two, one indeed which echoes both the earlier ones. The Greeks burst into Priam's chambers:

> fit via vi; rumpunt aditus primosque trucidant
> immissi Danai et late loca milite complent.
> non sic, aggeribus ruptis cum spumeus amnis
> exiit oppositasque evicit gurgite moles,
> fertur in arva furens cumulo camposque per omnis
> cum stabulis armenta trahit.
>
> (II.494–499)

The invasion, again seen by Aeneas, is like a river bursting its banks, an irresistible force sweeping all before it. The simile recalls the way in which the Greeks had first appeared to Aeneas at his father's house. Furthermore, its language echoes the description of the winds fanning the flame (*flamma furentibus Austris,* 304) and the torrent (*torrens,* 305) and reminds us again of the similarity in destructive power of fire and water.

One other, if minor, simile derived from natural forces occurs in book II. The plight of Hecuba and her daughters-in-law around the altar of the inner shrine of Priam's palace is compared to that of doves in a storm:

> praecipites atra ceu tempestate columbae
> (II.516)

Brief though the simile is its use of *tempestas* recalls the storm of book I.[7] Just before Troy's fall Hecuba and her daughters-in-law were like Aeneas and his men before the onslaught of the sea storm, helpless victims. Hecuba's clinging to the altar in a pious but vain hope of mercy was similar to Aeneas' first appearance in the *Aeneid,* where we find him in an attitude of prayer (I. 92 ff). In narrating Hecuba's action, Aeneas' language draws upon a common motif for eliciting pity, but the effect on the reader of Aeneas' simile is deepened because it recalls Aeneas' own attitude, at the same time it shows the reader

---

[7] See also pp. 12, 55.

how passive a victim Aeneas himself is in these first books of the *Aeneid*.

In book II the similes of nature's violence are all used to compare the invasion of the Greeks to the catastrophes of nature, and the point of view is always that of the victim who is incapable of responding in any other way than by passively enduring the onslaught. Aeneas who narrates the events of book II sees a parallel between what he and his men endured off the coast of Sicily and what they had earlier endured when Troy fell. Both events in his eyes are senseless and incomprehensible, for the Greeks acted, as the similes make clear, in the fashion of unfathomable nature. This emphasis on the Trojan helplessness elicits, of course, pity from Dido and her court and ultimately from the reader; it suggests the innocence of the Trojans both at the hands of men and nature. Yet when the events of book II are carefully considered, it becomes evident that the Trojans share in the responsibility for their own destruction. They, too, acted incomprehensibly in bringing in, for example, the wooden horse, which is compared to a mountain (II. 15). The comparison recalls the mountain of Aeolus whence the devastating storm came; so, too, from this wooden horse, huge as a mountain, will come devastation.[8] Even Aeneas is not above reproach, for it requires his mother's intervention as well as that of Creusa to force him to obey the instructions of Hector. His madness and rage for battle prove ultimately disastrous for the Trojans with him.[9] If the similes are set against this background, we can see that they make an ironic comment on Aeneas himself. He is not wholly the innocent victim he appears to be.

But the similes have a further implication and one which sheds light on the storm scene of book I. Although the Greeks are compared to a violent eruption of nature, they are nonetheless men who act from fathomable motives of their own; they want to destroy Troy, end the war, and go home; all understandable motives. Furthermore, in book II (624–631) Aeneas sees the gods dismantling the city they had built. The Greeks and the gods act in concert, so that what is revealed, even to Aeneas, is that Troy fell in accord with some sort of divine plan; the Greeks are agents in some sense of the gods, even as the winds which churned the sea acted as Juno's agents. The similes, by connecting men and nature, suggest that the seemingly dark events in nature may be part of a divine plan and therefore ultimately comprehensible.

---

[8] Putnam has well-discussed this point, p. 6 ff.

[9] For a discussion of this point see my article in *P.Q.*, XLV (1966), 347–349, also chapter 2 of this book, pp. 63 ff.

The next appearance of a storm simile occurs in book IV. Anna
pleads Dido's cause to Aeneas who, in the face of the plea, remains
firm in his intention to leave:

> Talibus orabat, talisque miserrima fletus
> fertque refertque soror. sed nullis ille movetur
> fletibus, aut voces ullas tractabilis audit;
> fata obstant placidasque viri deus obstruit auris.
> ac velut annoso validam cum robore quercum
> Alpini Boreae nunc hinc nunc flatibus illinc
> eruere inter se certant; it stridor, et altae
> consternunt terram concusso stipite frondes;
> ipsa haeret scopulis et quantum vertice ad auras
> aetherias, tantum radice in Tartara tendit:
> haud secus adsiduis hinc atque hinc vocibus heros
> tunditur, et magno persentit pectore curas;
> mens immota manet, lacrimae volvuntur inanes.
>
> (IV.437–449)

The simile is connected not only with the storm similes but also with
those which concern trees. For the oak tree to which Aeneas is here
compared recalls the oak simile involving the Cyclopes in book III
(677–681) and the mountain ash used as an image of Troy in book II
(624–631). Important as the tree similes are here, I prefer to center
the discussion for the moment on the fact that the oak is attacked by a
storm.[10] Anna's pleas are comparable to the northwinds blowing from
the Alps which try to overthrow the oak—Aeneas' spirit. Although
swayed by the winds, the oak nevertheless remains fixed, clinging to its
cliff, firmly anchored by its deep roots. The simile conveys Aeneas'
resolution, badly battered as it is. But for the first time in this series of
similes we see the actions of a single person, Anna, as distinct from a
mass of people, compared to a natural force, and we also see the failure
of the force to cause devastation. A new element has been added to the
similes which employ natural phenomena as destructive agents, and
that is deep-rooted firmness on the part of the thing attacked; passivity
has become patient endurance. In the context of book IV, Aeneas'
resolve is helped by the fates and gods; these are his deep roots, for
Aeneas, even as a tree, would not be able without aid to withstand
such a gale as Anna raises. He is lashed, as the end of the passage
makes clear, even as the oak tree is. The simile marks an advance
from the passivity of previous similes and when we next see Aeneas

---

[10] See also pp. 80 ff.

described as attacked by a natural force (in book X) a further advance will have been made. Significantly only Aeneas in the entire course of the *Aeneid* successfully sustains an attack which in a simile is compared to an attack of nature.

The comparison of the action of a single human being to an elemental and natural force recurs in book V where the almost-beaten Entellus recovers his strength and rains blows on Dares:

> nec mora nec requies: quam multa grandine nimbi
> culminibus crepitant, sic densis ictibus heros
> creber utraque manu pulsat versatque Dareta.
> (V.458–460)

In the context of the fight between Entellus and Dares, the older and supposedly weaker man turns out to be the victor. From the blow which almost destroys him he recovers to go on to victory. Entellus is an analogue to Aeneas, for like Aeneas he too has been buffeted; but unlike Aeneas, in the tree simile of book IV, Entellus emerges from that buffeting as the aggressor. His achievement foreshadows the development of Aeneas in the last six books. From the passive victim of the storm in book I Aeneas becomes eventually a storm cloud (books X and XII)[11] able to rain blows on his enemies.

With this simile the storm imagery of the first six books ends. All of the similes echo the storm scene in book I. But as the similes progress a change is observable in that the storm changes from a symbol of a mass of people—as in book II—and the victims are no longer passive recipients forced to endure the blows of the senseless elements. The storm becomes localized around one individual and the victim can endure undestroyed and ultimately turn into a storm himself. As the storm similes recur in greater profusion in the last six books these motifs will be paralleled until they reach their climax in book XII.

In book VII two important similes based on the violence of nature occur; both continue motifs found in earlier similes; both complement each other; and both derive from the storm of book I:[12]

> non iam certamine agresti
> stipitibus duris agitur sudibusve praeustis,
> sed ferro ancipiti decernunt atraque late

---

[11] See also pp. 38 ff., 124 ff.

[12] For an excellent discussion of these similes and their position in the structure of book VII, see Otis, pp. 325–328. See also E. Fränkel, "Some Aspects of the Structure of *Aeneid* VII," *Journal of Roman Studies*, XXXV (1945), 1–14.

horrescit strictis seges ensibus, aeraque fulgent
sole lacessita et lucem sub nubila iactant:
fluctus uti primo coepit cum albescere vento,
paulatim sese tollit mare et altius undas
erigit, inde imo consurgit ad aethera fundo.

(VII.523–530)

The simile compares the appearance of the struggle of Trojan and
Latin youth—the struggle which heralds the outbreak of the war—to
a seascape stirred up by winds. The simile emphasizes the appearance
of things; it is not the youths themselves who are being compared,
but their massed appearance as weapon-bearing men. The situation
described needs some unravelling. The Latin youths excited by the
death of Silvia's pet deer and the Trojan youth in defense of Ascanius,
the unwitting slayer of the deer, turn to weapons of iron and bronze.
The wheat fields bristle now with weapons which glitter in the sun
and at the same time disturb the light; the calm, natural appearance
of the wheat field has been transformed into a battlefield; and even the
natural light is affected by the transformation, as though the gleam of
the weapons were trying to rival the sun. Then comes the simile which
compares this scene on land to the changing appearance of the sea
stirred up by the winds so that first whitecaps appear and then the
waves reach higher and higher until in a mountainous rush the sea
seems to rise even to the heavens. The sea gradually undergoes a
change analogous to that which the land endures. But the details of
the simile do not function in a one-to-one relationship with the details
of the scene. At the start the winds are comparable to the men rushing
to arms, but then the sea itself in its upward thrust becomes like
the thrust of the men's weapons. The emphasis of the simile lies in the
transformation of nature, a transformation which reaches from the lowest depths to highest heaven. The point of view of both the scene and
the simile is that of one standing at a distance observing the change
and so perceiving the horrendous quality of the change. The simile
drawn from the phenomena of nature both emphasizes the changed
appearance of the land and affords a moral comment on the reason
for that change. Seen from a distance, the darkling plain on which
the Latin and Trojan youths gleam in their battle array is like a sea
transformed by winds; but upon reflection we perceive that this is a
similarity only of appearance, for men are culpable as nature is not.
By using metonymy to describe the scene—the men described in terms
of their weapons—and by employing the point of view of an observer
at some distance, and by using the same point of view in the simile,

Vergil dramatically shifts from cause to effect to illuminate his scene.

The use of the changed sea as the vehicle for the simile obviously recalls the description of the rising storm of book I. But the significant fact is that the land is compared to the sea, land changed by the changed appearance of men; the land has become the passive victim of the onslaught. Although the point was implicit in earlier similes, Vergil here makes it explicit for the first time. The simile is further related to those of book II which described the Greeks as a violent force of nature; the Trojan and Latin youths act as the Greeks did and just as elemental forces of nature do. But a difference is here discernible: for the first time in a simile the Trojans are associated with the enemy, unlike the similes of book II where the points of comparison were scrupulously confined to the Greeks alone.[13]

The power of the simile and the passage as a whole comes both from its skilful employment in book VII and also from the echoes of similar scenes and similes. Men on both sides have become a natural force bent on the destruction of nature itself. The fact that it is the Italian land which is about to be devastated by men who should know better underscores the poignancy of the simile and indicates to some degree how justified Vergil was in declaring at the opening of book VII *maius opus moveo* (45).[14]

Complementary to this simile is the second depicting a rock or cliff or promontory against which the waves of the sea dash. It is used to describe Latinus' attitude toward the Latins who favor war against the Trojans:

> certatim regis circumstant tecta Latini;
> ille velut pelago rupes immota resistit,
> ut pelagi rupes magno veniente fragore,
> quae sese multis circum latrantibus undis
> mole tenet; scopuli nequiquam et spumea circum
> saxa fremunt laterique inlisa refunditur alga.
> (VII.585–590)

In terms of the simile, the chief points are obvious: Latinus' resistance is like the *rupes* which remains *immota* and is steadfast because of its own weight, despite the waves and their noise (i.e., the people). The

---

[13] Note that in book II the Trojans were disguised as Greeks, implying thereby their share in the responsibility for the fall of Troy. So in book VII the Trojans and Latins are involved in what happens as active agents.

[14] The simile of the sea transformed is in harmony with the theme of the book: the land transformed by the (civil) war of men. This motif governs all the action and descriptions of the book.

use of the participle *latrantibus* (barking) arises from the din suggested by *fragore* in the previous line, but it conveys as well the notion of the yapping of dogs, and so underlines the noisy dog-like harassing of the people. The next two lines continue the image of sound but only imply the cause through the use of the transferred epithet *spumea* and the verb *refunditur*. By such indirection Vergil compels the reader to supply the full sequence of cause and effect in order that he may more vividly sense the similarity between the noise of the people and that of waves dashing on rocks and perceive the steadfastness of Latinus in the face of the people clamoring for war.

But the simile serves other purposes as well as simply describing Latinus before his people. The simile echoes the simile of Neptune-as-wise-statesman in book I, as critics have noted.[15] But now Vergil reverts to the more familiar use of the simile, for the noisy raging of men is now compared to the storm-tossed sea. Furthermore, its position in book VII, that is as the fourth and final simile in a series which marks the devastating effect of Allecto's activity, is comparable to the position of the simile used of Neptune in book I. The reason for the change of the simile as well as for its position is clear enough: Vergil emphasizes thereby how vast a difference exists between Latinus and Neptune, for the king of the Latins is unable to rule the spirit of his people; circumstances force Latinus to surrender all control and, as he admits in language which continues the sea simile (*frangimur . . . ferimurque procella, . . . omnisque in limine portus*—(594–598), he is broken, even though his attitude does not change. The context, the language, and the parallels with the Neptune passage of book I bring a terrible poignancy to Latinus' plight: Latinus is not a god of the sea; his people are not sea waves obedient to him.

But the echo, too, of the simile used of Aeneas in book IV, the storm-tossed oak simile, also is heard. Latinus not only is not like Neptune, he is also not like Aeneas. The success of the simile used of Latinus derives from the cumulative effect of the storm similes, and here we can see as clearly as one could wish how Vergil employs the simile as a part of his reverberating technique.

Two similes used of the troops Clausus leads forth for the Latin cause juxtapose a storm at sea and grain fields scorched by the sun:

> quam multi Libyco volvuntur marmore fluctus
> saevus ubi Orion hibernis conditur undis,

---

[15] Otis, pp. 327–328.

vel cum sole novo densae torrentur aristae
aut Hermi campo aut Lyciae flaventibus arvis.
(VII.718–721)

These alternative similes underscore motifs already noticed in the similes of book VII. First, the men in their movement are like the waves of the sea laboring under a wintry storm, a comparison which both describes their present appearance and implies their future storm-like qualities. Further, in their bristling, martial appearances the men look like so many ears of grain in a wheat field. But the simile carries a latent, ominous note, for grain fields are eventually harvested and so, too, will these men be cut down; but their harvester will be the god of war. Furthermore, to juxtapose sea and land reinforces the ironic quality already noticed in earlier similes of book VII—men who change the land into a sea of battle eventually suffer for the perversion of nature's world.

The first simile of book IX recalls that of book VII, the one just mentioned. Taken together the two are worthy of comment. It describes the army of the Latins converging on the field outside the Trojan camp:

Iamque omnis campis exercitus ibat apertis
dives equum, dives pictai vestis et auri—

.   .   .   .   .   .   .   .   .   .   .   .

ceu septem surgens sedatis amnibus altus
per tacitum Ganges aut pingui flumine Nilus
cum refluit campis et iam se condidit alveo.
(IX.25–26; 30–32)

The parts of the armies are like the streams which become the Ganges and the Nile and the whole army is like the broad rivers themselves, especially like the swollen Nile which overflows its channel. Although the simile itself conveys no scene of destruction, that idea is implicit within it, for swollen rivers are capable of being a force hostile to the neighboring lands. But more important, the use of rivers to describe a hostile army echoes the simile of book II (304–308) where the Greek force invading Troy was comparable to the raging torrent. The overflowing Nile suggests the devastation possible. The effect of the simile is not only to describe the Latin forces converging on the Trojan camp, but also to establish a link between the Latins and the Greeks. Potentially the Latins offer a threat to the Trojans that the Greeks once realized against Troy. So the first simile of the last third of the *Aeneid,* like the first one of the book where the struggle between the Trojans and the Latins begins in earnest, hints through its reminiscence of the past at the danger that lies ahead and implies that history repeats itself.

Book IX also contains one of the most touching similes in the *Aeneid,* that used to compare the dead Euryalus to a flower cut by the plow or poppies pummelled by a rainstorm:

> volvitur Euryalus leto, pulchrosque per artus
> it cruor inque umeros cervix conlapsa recumbit:
> purpureus veluti cum flos succisus aratro
> languescit moriens, lassove papavera collo
> demisere caput pluvia cum forte gravantur.
>
> (IX.433–437)

Otis has well observed that Vergil's use of the Catullan simile is a remarkable illustration of how he gives emotional vitality to his characters and episodes.[16] The simile's occurrence in the midst of the action underscores the significance of the destruction of Euryalus. His death appears as wanton and as senseless as the cutting down of the flower; Euryalus appears as the passive victim of external forces. But when we realize that Euryalus has a share in bringing about his own death and that his destruction will in turn be the proximate cause of the death of Nisus, we perceive that the simile serves an ironic function.[17] Euryalus is not simply a passive victim like the flower or the poppy. The simile in itself permits us to mourn the loss of the beauty of Euryalus, but its context permits us to judge how really wanton was Euryalus' death, even more wanton than the destruction of a flower, for had Euryalus not been led by his greed for glory he would not have been trapped and destroyed by the Latins; the glory of his youthful daring would have been employed in better, more fruitful ways.

But the significance of the simile is not yet exhausted. It is to be noted that the plow and the storm are equated, and, although both are necessary for the fruitfulness of the land, from the point of view of the poppy both are equally destructive. But to Vergil's audience there is a difference, for a plow unlike a rainstorm implies human agency and serves a purpose in which flowers, however beautiful, may be expendable. The plowing of the land is a necessity for its cultivation and the

---

[16] Otis, pp. 388–389.

[17] For a discussion of Euryalus' responsibility in his own death, see Otis, pp. 349–350. See also the discussion in this book, pp. 65 ff.

flower may well be destroyed in the process. This implicit notion reinforces the irony of the simile, for such a person as Euryalus had, in a sense, to be cut down for the civilization Aeneas is to found.

The comparison of human activity with natural disaster continues in book IX with the simile used in conjunction with the Trojan's defensive attack on the Latins:

> quantus ab occasu veniens pluvialibus Haedis
> verberat imber humum, quam multa grandine nimbi
> in vada praecipitant, cum Iuppiter horridus Austris
> torquet aquosam hiemem et caelo cava nubila rumpit.
> (IX.668–671)

Ascanius has successfully killed his first enemy.[18] Apollo approved the deed but enjoined him from further fighting. Because of Ascanius' act and the intervention of the god, the Trojans take heart and fight valiantly from within the walls of their camp. The simile likens the hail of arms and stones upon the shields and weapons of the attacking Latins to a wintry rainstorm. Echoing the storm scene of book I, the simile also alludes to Entellus' defeat of Dares (cf. V. 458–460), for the situation of the Trojans is comparable to that of Entellus, and like him, they take heart and go on to fight. Further, the Trojans are not the passive victims they once were; their activity has made them into the rainstorm themselves. Observe too that the god mentioned in the simile is Jupiter. The usage is appropriate in meteorological passages, but its use also suggests that the Trojans are in some way aligned with the will of Jupiter; it is as though by becoming like rain clouds they have become instruments of the divine will.

Book X has an array of similes based on the violence of nature. Just before Jupiter's concluding speech at the council of the gods at the beginning of book X occurs the following:

> Talibus orabat Juno, cunctique fremebant
> caelicolae adsensu vario, ceu flamina prima
> cum deprensa fremunt silvis et caeca volutant
> murmura venturos nautis prodentia ventos.
> (X.96–99)

Juno has just finished her speech in reply to Venus and the murmuring of the assembled gods is like the gale which blows through the woods and betrays the coming storm to sailors. The simile effectively

---

[18] See also pp. 15, 40.

depicts the behavior of the gods who are blown in alternate directions
by the speeches of Venus and Juno; they appear at the mercy of any
persuasive speech, powerless to act of their own volition. But the simile
also foreshadows the decision of Jupiter to give aid and comfort to
neither Trojan nor Latin. The gale here described is different from
earlier winds in the similes of the *Aeneid,* in that it foretells the coming storm but is not the storm itself. Although the simile does not
explicitly say so, in the light of the previous similes we augur that the
"coming winds" are to be destructive. These threatening overtones of
the simile anticipate Jupiter's decision that every man in that day's
battle must face the "coming storms" alone, that is to say, he must
determine his own fate. But the obscure murmuring of winds warns
sailors to take precautions, and it is the Trojans, far more than the
Latins, who have experienced the sea. The passage therefore suggests
that the outcome for Latin and Trojan may well differ. But men,
in any event, through their own actions become agents of the cosmic
purpose.

Upon Aeneas' return in book X two related similes occur:

> Iamque in conspectu Teucros habet et sua castra
> stans celsa in puppi, clipeum cum deinde sinistra
> extulit ardentem. clamorem ad sidera tollunt
> Dardanidae e muris, spes addita suscitat iras,
> tela manu iaciunt, quales sub nubibus atris
> Strymoniae dant signa grues atque aethera tranant
> cum sonitu, fugiuntque Notos clamore secundo.
> at Rutulo regi ducibusque ea mira videri
> Ausoniis, donec versas ad litora puppis
> respiciunt totumque adlabi classibus aequor.
> ardet apex capiti cristisque a vertice flamma
> funditur et vastos umbo vomit aureus ignis:
> non secus ac liquida si quando nocte cometae
> sanguinei lugubre rubent, aut Sirius ardor
> ille sitim morbosque ferens mortalibus aegris
> nascitur et laevo contristat lumine caelum.

> (X.260–275)

The two similes again complement each other. One describes the
response of the Trojans to the sight of Aeneas and the other justifies
that response by describing Aeneas in his armor. The Trojans' hopes
and courage for battle are renewed by the return of their leader. The
Servian commentary on line 265 observes that not the cast of the weapons but the clamor of the Trojans is being compared to the cranes.[19]

---

[19] *Servii Grammatici qui feruntur in Vergilii Carmina Commentarii,* eds. G. Thilo
et H. Hagen, II (Leipzig: B. G. Teubner, 1884), *ad.* 265, p. 420.

This may be the case, but the Dardanians do not leave their walls, only their weapons do, for the siege of the Trojan camp is not raised until 604–605. The missiles hurled by the Trojans seem more logically to be the point of comparison, and it is their whistling through the air as well as the shouts of the men which sounds like the Strymonian cranes. The significance of the cranes in this simile I shall leave until the next chapter;[20] for the moment it is enough to note that the cranes herald the storm. With the return of Aeneas, the Trojans, in effect, have become the storm which will eventually burst upon the Latins. Hence it is that the clamor is given the epithet *secundus,* favorable.

Aeneas in his armor is compared to two natural phenomena which were thought to herald disaster: comets and the dog star, Sirius.[21] The simile does not come unannounced in the *Aeneid*. In book VIII his armor had been similarly compared:

> miraturque interque manus et bracchia versat
> terribilem cristis galeam flammasque vomentem,
> fatiferumque ensem, loricam ex aere rigentem,
> sanguineam, ingentem, qualis cum caerula nubes
> solis inardescit radiis longeque refulget;
>
> (VIII.619–623)

To compare the armor glowing ruddy as the sky does when the clouds diffuse the rays of the sun suggests simultaneously the might of the sun and the threat of the clouds; both ideas are symbolized by Aeneas' armor. But in book X Aeneas in his armor is compared not to the sun but to a comet or a star, celestial phenomena commonly regarded as heralds of doom. Through the changed terms of the simile the armed Aeneas is seen as the bearer of destruction to his enemies, surrounded by an awesome divinity. These points are reinforced by the shift in the point of view, for it is through the eyes of the Latins that we see Aeneas.

But these similes of Aeneas as comet or star are not used of the hero alone. Two similar ones occur in relationship to the youthful Pallas. Indeed, the first of these similes immediately precedes the simile used of Aeneas' corselet. The juxtaposition is significant:

> Iamque adeo exierat portis equitatus apertis
> Aeneas inter primos et fidus Achates,
> inde alii Troiae proceres, ipse agmine Pallas

[20] See pp. 57 ff.
[21] Otis, p. 355 and the footnote where he cites Apollonius' use of a similar comparison (*Arg*. III. 956–961) and Homer, *Iliad* 5.4 ff. Otis does not go into the ramifications of the simile.

> in medio chlamyde et pictis conspectus in armis,
> qualis ubi Oceani perfusus Lucifer unda,
> quem Venus ante alios astrorum diligit ignis,
> extulit os sacrum caelo tenebrasque resolvit.
>
> (VIII.585–591)

Pallas in his chlamys and arms among the chiefs appears like Lucifer who lifts his sacred head and casts out the darkness from the heavens. The simile emphasizes the handsomeness of the young leader while also pointing up his intimate connection with the Trojan enterprise of casting out the darkness of the Latins' cause. His appearance on the side of the Trojans heralds the success of their mission, for the union between Pallas' father and Aeneas is the prologue to the ultimate union of the native Latins and the Trojans. As light-bearer Pallas is the symbol of the future of Latium.

Moreover, the simile anticipates the fate of Pallas himself. He will, we know, be cut down, even as the morning star at last fades before the brilliance of the sun, for Venus' love for the star cannot prevent his succumbing to the brighter light. But before his death Pallas enjoys the brief glory of exhorting his men to noble battle. He, in that scene (X. 399 ff.), enflames his men by his own action; he sets them on fire, and like Lucifer shows them the light. The simile used to comment on his action makes the point emphatically clear:

> ac velut optato ventis aestate coortis
> dispersa immittit silvis incendia pastor,
> correptis subito mediis extenditur una
> horrida per latos acies Volcania campos,
> ille sedens victor flammas despectat ovantis:
> non aliter socium virtus coit omnis in unum
> teque iuvat, Palla.
>
> (X.405–411)

The simile is connected with both that of book VIII and with the similes of the destructive forces of nature, especially fire. But it draws upon the pastoral world, and what the shepherd does here is burn off the field in order to make it more verdant. The reference to the shepherd echoes the shepherd simile of book II (304–308) used of Aeneas viewing the destruction of Troy.[22] But the change from the passive shepherd of book II to the active and beneficent one in book X marks how far the cause of the Aeneadae has advanced. Furthermore, the

---

[22] See also pp. 13 ff., 22 ff., 31, 64, 91, 101.

fire symbolizes the force of the allies of Aeneas rather than his enemies and it is a refining fire which destroys the opposing Latins. In
enflaming his men Pallas becomes truly Lucifer.

But to return for a final glance at the Lucifer simile of Pallas and
the cloud simile of Aeneas. The juxtaposition is not accidental. Pallas
is both like and unlike Aeneas. He does not have the wealth of mature
experience Aeneas enjoys, nor the profound awareness which Aeneas
by the end of book VIII has attained. Nor should he. Younger than
the hero, he has yet to grow into the fulfillment of his heroic promise.
Like the morning star, he announces the coming of light, but also like
the morning star he will never realize it himself. He does not, hence,
share Aeneas' fate, though he is intimately involved in that fate, for it
is because of Pallas that Aeneas finally slays Turnus.

Yet the morning star, Lucifer, when it first appears, shines forth
more brilliantly than does the sun, which appears in early morning as
a reddish cloud. It is for this reason that Vergil in book VIII has juxta-
posed the two similes—Pallas as shining morning star; Aeneas' armor
as red-glowing cloud. Pallas will ultimately fade away, whereas Aeneas
will finally emerge as the sun itself does. A further point can also be
observed about the simile of the armor and its relationship to a glowing cloud. Aeneas at this point in the tale has not yet proven himself
in the war where the final test of all he has learned is to be found. He
gives promise, but he is still in a sense clouded over. He has not yet
appeared in his full, awesome light. His armor is his cloud; what he
does with the armor remains to be told.

This use of the cloud imagery with Aeneas is connected with the
cloud which surrounded him in book I. There his mother, Venus, in
order to conceal his approach to Carthage and Dido, enveloped him
and Achates in a cloud of invisibility. Not until it was safe for him did
he emerge, and then he emerged resplendent as Apollo. In that book,
as in book VIII, his mother is the agent for giving Aeneas the protection he needs. But the cloud of book I becomes the armor of book VIII.
Through the armor Aeneas will at last be able to fend for himself and
show himself as he is. The promise of book I is fulfilled by book VIII.
Aeneas must now begin to realize himself as a leader of men, as a
bearer of civilization. But the ultimate revelation of himself is not to
occur until the very end of book XII when he kills Turnus. In that
scene, as we shall see, he justifies himself as the sun and does so because
of Pallas, Lucifer, the morning star, the harbinger of light.

A simile in book X describes the Trojan and Latin battle lines:

> magno discordes aethere venti
> proelia ceu tollunt animis et viribus aequis;
> non ipsi inter se, non nubila, non mare cedit;
> anceps pugna diu, stant obnixa omnia contra:
> haud aliter Troianae acies aciesque Latinae
> concurrunt, haeret pede pes densusque viro vir.
>
> (X.356–361)

The simile is that of battling winds used to describe strong men at war, and so recalls the personified winds of the first simile of the *Aeneid*, the winds of the storm simile of book II (416–419), the simile of the sea stirred by winds in book VII (523–530), and it occurs immediately after the telling phrases:

> expellere tendunt
> nunc hi, nunc illi: certatur limine in ipso
> Ausoniae.
>
> (X.354–356)

The men in their fighting are like the winds which fight over the Italian countryside. The comparison of the strength of men to a force of nature is a familiar one by now in the *Aeneid*. Because it echoes those earlier passages the simile and its context acquires a power beyond what they could by themselves sustain, for the verbal echoes also echo the emotional and moral implications of the earlier passages. The moral irresponsibility of both Trojans and Latins has been massively explored in book IX. In a sense, this simile concludes that exploration and at the same time it prepares for the description of the stasis which occurs at 755–761, after which the tide of battle changes slowly in favor of the Trojans. Significantly, this is the only simile in the entire *Aeneid* which deliberately compares the men to wind alone. It can afford to do so because of its echoes of previous similes. Further, it is the last simile in which both Trojans and Latins are joined in common guilt.[23]

Three more similes based on the destruction caused by a natural force occur in book X, which both echo previous similes and confirm their implications. The three are connected; two describe Aeneas and one Mezentius. The first,

---

[23] Only once more are Trojans and Latins combined in any simile. It occurs at XII. 715–724 and is discussed in chapter 7, pp. 132 ff.

talia per campos edebat funera ductor
Dardanius torrentis aquae vel turbinis atri
more furens.

(X.602–604)

describes the havoc Aeneas wreaks in clearing the way from the landing stage to the beleaguered Trojan camp. He is the bearer of death to
his enemies just as a torrent or a black whirlwind is. He is now not
simply the harbinger of doom, he is the agent of it. Aeneas has become
like the Greeks in book II and like the winds which once had bela-
bored him. No longer is he a passive victim, but rather he has become
similar to a natural force. This particular passage marks the change in
Aeneas which came about when he put on the armor Vulcan had
made for him. Comparable to the Greeks at Troy and to Entellus in
Sicily, Aeneas in gaining his heroic stature and refining his strength,
fulfills, or perhaps more accurately, begins to fulfill the promise
Entellus foreshadowed.

The next simile continues a motif found in the one just discussed.
Vergil turns the scene from Aeneas to concentrate on Mezentius. The
simile occurs at the beginning of Mezentius' *aristeia:*

ille (velut rupes vastum quae prodit in aequor,
obvia ventorum furiis expostaque ponto,
vim cunctam atque minas perfert caelique marisque
ipsa immota manens) prolem Dolichaonis Hebrum
sternit humi, cum quo Latagum Palmumque fugacem,
sed Latagum saxo atque ingenti fragmine montis
occupat os faciemque adversam, poplite Palmum
succiso volvi segnem sinit, armaque Lauso
donat habere umeris et vertice figere cristas.

(X.693–701)

The rainstorm which along with other elements assails the rock is not
unlike the storm cloud that has been used about Aeneas. But, in addition, the fact that a rock is used as a comparison for Mezentius echoes
the rock or cliff used in book VII to describe Latinus' attitude. The
suggestion is that like Latinus, Mezentius himself will be found not to
be a stalwart, everlasting Gibraltar; he too will be crushed, and by
Aeneas. But the context of the simile appears incongruous with the
simile itself, for cliffs after all do not lay about them as Mezentius does.
(Note that Mezentius' strength or force is not being compared here,
only the man, *ille.*) Cliffs or promontories are notoriously passive as

the simile makes clear. No such incongruity existed in the simile in book VII (585–590), where it was an attitude and not a man that was described. This incongruity, as well as the echo of the simile used of Latinus in book VII, suggests that Vergil wants his readers to discriminate between the two men: Latinus, for all his passivity, comes off the better; Mezentius' strength is the embodiment of his character which is hard and unfeeling like a rock, just as his actions in his *aristeia* and his scorn of the gods show.[24] Such is Vergil's subtle manipulation of these devices.

The third of these similes in the last portion of book X compares the hail of weapons to a heavy rainstorm. It is a complex one and deserves along with its context close scrutiny:

> proripuit iuvenis seseque immiscuit armis,
> iamque adsurgentis dextra plagamque ferentis
> Aeneae subiit mucronem ipsumque morando
> sustinuit; socii magno clamore sequuntur,
> dum genitor nati parma protectus abiret,
> telaque coniciunt perturbantque eminus hostem
> missilibus. furit Aeneas tectusque tenet se.
> ac velut effusa si quando grandine nimbi
> praecipitant, omnis campis diffugit arator
> omnis et agricola, et tuta latet arce viator
> aut amnis ripis aut alti fornice saxi,
> dum pluit in terris, ut possint sole reducto
> exercere diem: sic obrutus undique telis
> Aeneas nubem belli, dum detonet omnis,
> sustinet et Lausum increpitat Lausoque minatur:
>                                                   (X.796–810)

Aeneas has just wounded Mezentius, who is helped off the field by his son Lausus, and whose companions hurl their weapons upon Aeneas. Aeneas in turn protects himself by withdrawing from the aggressive attack until the fury of the allies has spent itself. The simile recalls the earlier one (IX. 668–671) which compared weapons to hailstones both in appearance and sound. Indeed, the phrase *nubem belli* clearly states the point, but Aeneas, however, is here battered by the rain of weapons. That such a simile should occur after one which described Aeneas himself as a storm cloud may appear odd. But if we examine it closely, the oddness, I think, disappears.

---

[24] Of course Mezentius' death has a certain poignancy about it, for he has one virtue, his love for his son. But that is not enough to redeem him for the new society. Vergil wants the reader to perceive this and also to comprehend at what cost society advances.

The simile involves the figures of human beings who seek shelter until the storm has passed and who then return to the day's business. For the first time in this series of similes, the simile describes a defensive action of a human being. The implication is that even a victim of a destructive attack need not be wholly passive, for he has recourse to trying to protect himself from the elements. But, more significantly, this simile makes explicit for the first time what has been implicit in the previous similes, namely, that natural events, even those of a catastrophic nature, finally wear themselves out and end; so also does the fury and power of a man's attack cease. When it does, if the victim has husbanded his strength so far as he can, he in turn has a greater advantage over his exhausted enemy. Prudent endurance is what it is necessary to learn, just as Aeneas has learned it in the course of his toils from Troy to Latium. Even in the midst of his anger (*furit* 802) he does not forget his lessons, as the rest of line 802 implies.

But what does this have to do with Aeneas as rain cloud? Aeneas, like Mezentius, will eventually dissipate his wrath and fury, and like the rain cloud they too shall pass. The simile anticipates the end of Aeneas' anger. The defensive attitude he adopts here is the first step in the final change he will undergo in book XII. He will not be concerned, finally, with venting his anger on a multitude of men, but with one alone, Turnus. But even that will at last turn as he makes the final sacrifice at the end of the epic. Like the human beings in the simile, he can then go about his proper business—making peace and laying the foundations of a new civilization. The simile indicates how deeply Aeneas has profited from the past, and thereby increases the accumulated significance of such similes.

In book XI, the first of two similes invoking natural forces occurs at the end of Venulus' report to the Latin people of his unsuccessful mission to Diomedes:

> Vix ea legati, variusque per ora cucurrit
> Ausonidum turbata fremor, ceu saxa morantur
> cum rapidos amnis, fit clauso gurgite murmur
> vicinaeque fremunt ripae crepitantibus undis.
> (XI.296–299)

The murmuring of the people, unlike that of the gods in book X, is compared to the sound which the rush of water makes over a rocky stream bed, possibly because men are terrestrial creatures and do not dwell in the upper reaches of the heavens. The importance of the simile lies not only in its adequate comparison of sounds, but also, and more importantly, because it prepares the way for a later simile in book XI where the Latin people are compared to the ebbing and flowing sea. The connection of the Latins with moving water is the chief point.

The complementary simile describes the Latin people, hard pressed by the Trojans as they turn and rush toward the gates of their city. Their movement is compared to the movement of the sea:

> qualis ubi alterno procurrens gurgite pontus
> nunc ruit ad terram scopulosque superiacit unda
> spumeus extremamque sinu perfundit harenam,
> nunc rapidus retro atque aestu revoluta resorbens
> saxa fugit litusque vado labente relinquit:
> bis Tusci Rutulos egere ad moenia versos,
> bis reiecti armis respectant terga tegentes.
> tertia sed postquam congressi in proelia totas
> implicuere inter se acies legitque virum vir,
> tum vero et gemitus morientum et sanguine in alto
> armaque corporaque et permixti caede virorum
> semianimes volvuntur equi, pugna aspera surgit.
> (XI.624–635)

The ebb and flow of the sea appears as predictable as the movement of masses of men in combat. But in this simile the explicit statement of the destructive capacity of the sea is absent, unlike either the wind simile of book X (356–361) or the earlier similes of book VII (523–530; 585–590; 718–721) where the sea was also used to describe men *en masse*. However, the movement of men and the tides of the sea are not the same; men do not endlessly move back and forth. The point is emphasized by the lines immediately following the simile. Combat is joined; the battlefield becomes a scene of carnage, jumbled, confused, groaning as the quoted lines indicate, and bitter battle surges up. Although the language used to describe the scene is appropriate to a hostile sea, the scene is nonetheless one on land, and the hostility comes from the men themselves; they have become the raging sea. In their actions they have realized the first simile of hostile nature in book VII (523–530) which was elaborated in the similes of books IX and X. By comparing the movement of men to the motion of the sea, Vergil is able to use the other aspects of his sea similes as the basis for his description of the battle. The metaphorical description of the general battle shows the consequences, as it were, of the sea-people correspondence contained in the simile. The passage gains its power, then, from the adroit placing of the simile, summoning as it does previous passages in the *Aeneid*.

What then are the conclusions of this survey of similes of destructive natural forces? In themselves the similes compare in various ways the action of men to the hostile elements in nature. They show repeatedly how often men's actions are as blind, heedless, and deadly as ever nature herself can be. At the same time, the similes also imply that the raging fury of men is like the fury of the elements in that it eventually wears itself out. Unless they are madmen, men cannot stand to rage forever. Further, as the forces of nature attack both men and their homes, so also do men. The victims are worn down and eventually destroyed. But the irony of the similes clearly lies in the fact that men destroy the very thing they want to preserve. As the progression of similes from book VII marches onward, it becomes more and more evident that the land and its greatest product—the men themselves—are the victims of their own destructive force, the Trojans no less than the Latins. As the Trojans shared in the destruction of Troy, so also do the Latins share in the destruction of Latium. This is the tragedy of men who act blindly.

The similes echo the storm scene of book I and reflect upon that major event. The sea raging against Aeneas foretells the Latins raging against the Trojans. But at the same time the similes comparing men to sea storms reveal that the great sea storm anticipated the rage of the Latins and not the continuing hostility of nature. While the similes refer to the first book they do so with varying emphasis, highlighting now one thing, now another, in order to bring out the connection between nature and men. But Vergil complicates the matter even further by echoing connections between the similes themselves. All are tightly interwoven and so depend on each other as well as on their common source. As the similes occur, they show a change in their points of comparison. The Trojans move from passive victims to active agents, and a shift occurs from concentrating on a mass of men as hostile creatures to individual men. The change is clear in books II–V where the movement is from Greeks versus Trojans to Anna versus Aeneas or Dares versus Entellus. The same pattern is repeated in books VII–X, especially books IX and X which so frequently concern individual fighters. But then in book XI the similes of hostile nature are fewer and apply only to the Latins. By the end of book XI, the Latins have been placed in a position analogous to that of Aeneas and the remnant from Troy at the beginning of the poem. Vergil clearly does so in order to prepare for the flaring of these similes in book XII. It is a lull before the final storm.

Yet while all these things go on because of the similarity in appearance between men's actions and those of nature herself, the similes also imply a discrepancy between men and nature. The two are in a profound sense incommensurate. Men, unlike the hostile, destructive forces of nature, can be held responsible for the consequences of their actions. It is this discrepancy which lies, finally, at the heart of these similes and which allows them to become a moral commentary on men, for it is in the awareness of this discrepancy that we perceive the tragic quality which underlies man's folly.

## Benign Phenomena

Related to the similes of the destructive forces of nature is a small group describing either actions of various characters or the characters themselves in terms of celestial or natural phenomena. There is no connotation of destruction in these similes, and they occur always in circumstances benign to the cause of Aeneas and the Trojans.

A simile in book V compares to a meteor the arrow which Acestes shoots and which bursts into flame:

> namque volans liquidis in nubibus arsit harundo
> signavitque viam flammis tenuisque recessit
> consumpta in ventos, caelo ceu saepe refixa
> transcurrunt crinemque volantia sidera ducunt.
> (V.525–528)

The event is immediately seen by the Trojans as an omen of good fortune. But it is so only because of important previous events involving fire: as a good omen at the time of the departure from Troy and from Carthage.[25] When Aeneas tried to persuade Anchises to leave

---

[25] Otis, p. 275. As far as I know, and as he observes, he is the first to have noted the connection between Acestes' arrow and the comet omen of book II. See also Putnam, pp. 83–86.

Troy, his father at first refused, but at last consented when he saw Ascanius' head encircled with harmless flames (II. 679–686). At that point Anchises calls upon Jupiter for confirmation of the omen, and thunder sounds and a shooting star is seen. The fire which had destroyed Troy has become a benevolent guide to the remnant of Trojans. Similarly in book V fire appears to the Trojans in two guises. At the opening of the book, the Trojans upon sailing from Carthage see the flames of Dido's pyre, and their eyes are opened to what destruction they have escaped.

Acestes' arrow, however, is interpreted as simply a benign omen for the Trojans. The comparison to a meteor relates the sign to the heavens, and thereby indicates the favorable will of the gods. The meteor here serves the function supplied by the shooting star in the earlier episode of book II. But the fact that fire is used, even celestial fire indicative of the will of Jupiter, indicates as well the potential danger lurking in the future for the Trojans, for fire can be double-edged, and frequently is: at the same moment it can destroy and refine. Even as it destroyed Troy by refining the harmful qualities of Troy, so it will refine the Trojan remnant, for before the end of book V the old and fainthearted abandon Aeneas' enterprise in order to remain on Sicily.

That those unwilling to sail on with Aeneas should be allowed to remain with Acestes, the shade Anchises in a dream assures Aeneas. The way the shade leaves Aeneas is compared to smoke evaporating in clouds:

> dixerat et tenuis fugit ceu fumus in auras.
> (V.740)

Although the simile in its context is perfectly appropriate for describing the departure of a ghost, nevertheless the fact that smoke is used for the vehicle of the simile suggests that Anchises' words and Acestes' arrow are connected.[26] Anchises has come to instruct Aeneas who now learns that he must go to Italy, leaving a portion of his followers on Sicily, and he must seek his father in the underworld.

Although the simile is connected to others of book V, it has even a stronger connection with a brief one occurring in book II and

---

[26] Note that *tenuisque recessit / consumpta in ventos* (526–527) is echoed by *tenuis fugit ceu fumus in auras* (740). Note, too, that Aeneas immediately rekindles the fire and makes sacrifice (743–745).

repeated in book VI. Aeneas describes how he vainly tried to embrace the shade of Creusa after her words of farewell:

> ter conatus ibi collo dare bracchia circum;
> ter frustra comprensa manus effugit imago,
> par levibus ventis volucrique simillima somno.
> (II.792–794)

The simile of 794 beautifully conveys the lightness and evanescence of Creusa's ghost; she who once was solid reality to Aeneas has now become as ungraspable as the winds and a subject fit for dreams. That she should appear so after her comforting words to him (II. 776–789) adds poignancy to Aeneas' last experience of her, just as the smoke simile of book V adds a touch of pathos to Anchises' departure from Aeneas.

Not only does the smoke simile of book V recall that used of Creusa's shade, but it also anticipates the repetition of the same simile in book VI where it is used of Anchises' ghost (VI. 700–702 = II. 792–794). The poignancy of the meeting is again underscored. But this time the simile occurs, significantly, almost at the start of the meeting: before Anchises tells Aeneas of the future of his race and of Rome. Thus, though the meeting between father and son is poignant it nevertheless has a grander purpose than did that between Creusa and Aeneas. Yet, again, instruction is the keynote of the episode. By coupling similes of light wind or smoke with oral instruction, the similes and their contexts stress the fragility of speech, for words are but breath with significance. However it is in that very fact, i.e., that speech is meaningful air, that these similes, brief though they be, reverberate against the other kinds of winds used in the storm similes, for in these passages speech gives comfort and encouragement; it is as though Vergil were hinting through these similes and their contexts that not every movement of air leads to destruction and ruin. These similes are used of ghosts who tell Aeneas of some test he must undergo. Symbolically then, speech, light as air, conveys the heaviest responsibilities. Only in book XII will it be clear how serious an importance must be attached to so evanescent a thing as speech.

*Chapter 2*

# The World of Nature:
# Animals

In addition to the phenomena of nature, Vergil finds the animal world (bees, birds, ants, dolphins, snakes, bulls, wolves, and lions) a rich source for analogies with the actions of men. Twenty-nine animal similes appear in the *Aeneid* I–XI, but their frequency and use differ markedly between books I–VI and VII–XI: twelve animal similes occur in the first six books as against seventeen in the next five books.[1] In books I–VI appear the only snake similes of the *Aeneid,* two of which are in book II. Five similes compare groups of men to ants, flocks of birds, hives of bees, or schools of dolphins, and none of these similes describes the creatures in a hostile situation. Two similes involve wounded animals and one, predatory beasts. But, in books VII–XI, only three similes compare human beings to flocks of birds, and one to a wounded animal, whereas thirteen similes compare individual men to savage beasts. From these statistics alone it is evident that Vergil sharply distinguished between the animal similes in the two halves of his poem. Yet the two halves are connected, for clearly the one simile of predatory beasts in the first half is related to the thirteen similar similes in books VII–XI, just as the three similes which compare men to flocks of birds in books VII–XI are related to the six similes of the same type in the first six books.

But as the similes are scrutinized, the connections between both

---

[1] Six more animal similes appear in book XII and will be discussed in chapter 7, pp. 119 ff.

the first and last parts of the poem as well as between individual similes become evident and reveal a deliberate pattern. In order to examine these connections and their significance, I have divided the animal similes into two groups. The first employs nonpredatory animals and dominates in books I–VI; the second, dominant in the last part of the epic, compares men to savage beasts. Within each major division subdivisions occur, as will become clear. To turn then to the similes which employ as their vehicle bees, ants, dolphins, or birds.

Among the most famous similes in the *Aeneid* is that of the bees in book I:

> Corripuere viam interea, qua semita monstrat.
> iamque ascendebant collem, qui plurimus urbi
> imminet adversasque aspectat desuper arces.
> miratur molem Aeneas, magalia quondam,
> miratur portas strepitumque et strata viarum.
> instant ardentes Tyrii: pars ducere muros
> molirique arcem et manibus subvolvere saxa,
> pars optare locum tecto et concludere sulco;
> iura magistratusque legunt sanctumque senatum.
> hic portus alii effodiunt; hic alta theatris
> fundamenta locant alii, imanisque columnas
> rupibus excidunt, scaenis decora alta futuris.
> qualis apes aestate nova per florea rura
> exercet sub sole labor, cum gentis adultos
> educunt fetus, aut cum liquentia mella
> stipant et dulci distendunt nectare cellas,
> aut onera accipiunt venientum, aut agmine facto
> ignavum fucos pecus a praesepibus arcent;
> fervet opus redolentque thymo fragrantia mella.
> 'O fortunati, quorum iam moenia surgunt!'
>                                   (I.418–437)

The simile is a full-scale, "Homeric" simile which comments on the scene of the building of Carthage, as viewed by Aeneas who looks down on the activity from a nearby hill. The details of the bee simile correspond chiastically to the details of the previous description of the Carthaginians, i.e., the Carthaginians begin with their defensive measures, the description of the bees ends with a corresponding motif (423–424 and 434–435); the labor of the Carthaginians corresponds to the labor of the bees (426–429 and 431–434). The tone of the simile has a joy and exuberance about it which derives from the harmonious activity of the bees so that we transfer our pleasure from the bees to the men. Because of this transfer of emotion from one object to another, we tend to regard the bees as a social model against which we can judge human activity: men should be, we feel, like the bees who live and work in harmony.[2] We sympathize, in short, with Aeneas, and we feel the pathos he expresses in line 437.

But Vergil does not content himself with arousing our sympathy. Upon reflection, we become aware that Vergil uses the point of view of Aeneas and the bee simile to reveal something of the character of Aeneas, namely his self-pity. But we also perceive that Aeneas has not thought carefully about what he witnesses. To compare men to bees can at best be only superficial, for the harmonious action of the bees is impelled by their very nature, but no such impulse guides men to act in concord; only the will, consciously directed, can so move men. Aeneas sees only superficially, and his response is, therefore, partial so that he feels the pathos of his plight.

But the entire passage is not yet exhausted. To join in building a city such as Carthage is not for Aeneas. Indeed his arrival at Carthage will cause the cessation of activity: the hive will become disordered; its ruler will cease to trouble about it, preferring instead to concentrate attention on herself alone. The simile presages this ironic reversal in the reference to keeping the drones from the hive. To the Carthaginians, Aeneas and his Trojans will appear as drones who threaten the proper activity of the hive, and the Carthaginians themselves will form a hostile battle line to drive the Trojans from their precincts.

The simile illuminates not only the present behavior of the Carthaginians in building their city, but Aeneas' partial understanding of their behavior. It thus helps reveal a facet of Aeneas' character, a facet which must undergo a change before he can emerge as the hero of civilization. Further, the simile looks toward the future consequences of Aeneas' arrival in Carthage. With an economy of expression, Vergil achieves considerable connotative force from his simile.

A later simile comparing the Trojans to ants balances the bee simile. Aeneas has at last decided to leave Dido's court and her baneful love. The Trojans preparing for their departure are described:

> migrantis cernas totaque ex urbe ruentis:
> ac velut ingentem formicae farris acervum
> cum populant hiemis memores tectoque reponunt,
> it nigrum campis agmen praedamque per herbas

---

[2] Vergil similarly uses the image of the bee and hive in *Georgics* IV. But there, too, he exploits the dissimilarity between bees and men. See Otis, pp. 181–190 for *Georgics* IV and H. Dahlmann, "Der Bienenstaat in Vergils Georgika," *Akad. der wiss. Mainz*, (1954), 10, cited by Otis. On the bee simile of *Aeneid* I, see Otis, p. 65.

convectant calle angusto; pars grandia trudunt
obnixae frumenta umeris, pars agmina cogunt
castigantque moras, opere omnis semita fervet.
quis tibi tum, Dido, cernenti talia sensus,
quosve dabas gemitus, cum litora fervere late
prospiceres arce ex summa, totumque videres
misceri ante oculos tantis clamoribus aequor!

(IV.401–411)

The activity of the Trojans, like that of the Carthaginians in book I, is compared to the purposive activity of social insects. Both societies, like both kinds of insects, are busy furthering their own interests. Yet the ant simile, when considered in the light of the earlier bee simile, suggests by its language and point of view a difference in the way the two people are regarded. The context of the simile again reveals Vergil's manipulation of point of view. The subject of *cernas* in line 401 at first glance appears to be that of Vergil's audience, an omniscient observer of the scene, but the use of *tibi* and the vocative of *Dido* as well as the second person singular verbs in and following line 408 suggest that Dido is also in some way the subject of *cernas:* the reader's point of view and Dido's have merged. This ambiguity has an effect on the simile, for the simile not only describes the Trojans as ants busy about their work, a natural enough parallel, but also implies that their activity is a military operation causing the devastation of the land, as indeed it is from Dido's point of view. Like the ants, the Trojans seem to be struggling to strip the land and to store its produce as booty. Yet nothing in the account of the Trojans leaving Carthage implies that they treated Carthage as a defeated city capable of supplying booty; only Dido would believe it so.

The insects chosen to represent the two groups of men underscore the two different points of view, which in turn reveal aspects of the characters of Dido and Aeneas. The Trojans to Dido, whose love has turned to hatred, appear as ants—mean, insignificant creatures incapable of creating anything of worth for men, but capable of destruction; to Aeneas the Carthaginians were creating something not only useful for themselves but also for others, just as the bees distill honey for the use of others. Both Aeneas, in viewing the Carthaginians, and Dido, in gazing on the Trojans, suffer from not being fully aware of what they are viewing. Yet Aeneas reveals a generosity which Dido with her consuming hatred cannot foster.[3]

---

[3] For the discussion of Dido and Aeneas and the similes surrounding them see chapter 4, pp. 89 ff.

The next simile involving insects occurs in book VI:

> Interea videt Aeneas in valle reducta
> seclusum nemus et virgulta sonantia silvae,
> Lethaeumque domos placidas qui praenatat amnem.
> hunc circum innumerae gentes populique volabant:
> ac veluti in pratis ubi apes aestate serena
> floribus insidunt variis et candida circum
> lilia funduntur, strepit omnis murmure campus.
> (VI.703–709)

Again bees recur. The point made by the simile chiefly emphasizes the serenity of the blessed dead coming to drink of the river Lethe; the tone of the whole passage is one of idyllic peacefulness appropriate to the peaceful and purified dead. Vergil stresses one detail of bees, their murmuring, in order to suggest the soft voices of the purified souls, but by that detail he conveys the harmoniousness which the previous bee simile suggested.

Not only the use of bees for the vehicle of the simile, but other details of the passage recall the scene of book I where the Carthaginians appeared to Aeneas like bees. Again Aeneas looks down from above, again the scene is laid in a valley; the same mood of joy and sense of harmony is evoked. But the second bee simile differs from the first, and by its difference comments on the limitations of Aeneas' earlier vision of harmony.

The earlier simile, reflecting the description of the Carthaginians building their city, dwelt upon the daily round of human toil, of mortal affairs. Occurring at the end of the description, the simile's mood of harmony reflects upon the description, but also, in a sense, it is superimposed on the scene by Aeneas' vision. But how precarious or even false was the harmony, subsequent events revealed; and indeed this fragility was already suggested by the allusions to defensive measures, to the enemy without, that frame the description and the simile. This latent threat to harmony seems altogether to have escaped Aeneas' perception, though not the reader's.

In the later bee simile, on the other hand, the harmony itself is perceived immediately by Aeneas, although he does not know whence it comes. By its position in the narrative, the simile implies Aeneas' ignorance and prepares the way for the revelation to come. Anchises soon enlightens his son about the true meaning of what he sees and hears; and so Aeneas passes from ignorance to knowledge and a deeper understanding. There is no longer self-pity in him, but a readiness to go forth with the new knowledge that true harmony comes only from perfect knowledge, as in the realm of the blessed of the purified souls.

The simile of the bees in book VI complements, then, the simile of book I. By alluding to only one detail of the earlier simile, Vergil can concisely remind his audience of the effect and purpose of that simile in order to prepare the way for his portrayal of Aeneas' emotional and intellectual education. The repetition of the bees as the vehicle of the simile shows us how far Aeneas has come, intellectually, emotionally, and spiritually, from Carthage.

Significantly, too, when men or souls are compared to bees, it is Aeneas whose point of view we share; whereas with Dido we can only see men as ants. The point reveals that even in book I Aeneas distantly glimpsed that the harmony he saw spread before him was somehow connected with a cosmic harmony, and that men live best when they live in terms of it. But he discovers only through his spiritual education that this is really so. Such a glimpse is never vouchsafed Dido who can only view human activity as destructive to herself. Aeneas longs to build his city in order to realize as fully as possible the destiny laid upon him; Dido destroys her city in one gigantic act of self-immolation.

These three similes of insects who act in concert are not unlike a similar group which also describe a mass movement of men. Instead of insects, dolphins serve as the vehicle of the simile. Dolphins appear three times in the *Aeneid,* and the passages are all related. But in order to discuss the dolphins, it is first necessary to discuss another simile, that of the labyrinth with which the dolphin simile is first coupled.

In book V, a large part of which is concerned with teamwork, the Trojan boys in their maneuvers on horseback are described in the following passage:

> ut quondam Creta fertur Labyrinthus in alta
> parietibus textum caecis iter ancipitemque
> mille viis habuisse dolum, qua signa sequendi
> frangeret indeprensus et inremeabilis error;
> haud alio Teucrum nati vestigia cursu
> impediunt texuntque fugas et proelia ludo,
> delphinum similes qui per maria umida nando
> Carpathium Libycumque secant.
>
> (V.588–595)

In coupling the Cretan labyrinth with the sporting play of dolphins in the sea, Vergil shows us a single event from two different views. The boys are engaged in maneuvers which for the time being are harmless, but eventually in the course of the *Aeneid* such maneuvers will play a part in the deadly seriousness of warfare where an error will have grievous consequences. The Cretan labyrinth ominously anticipates this change. But the intricate movements of the Trojan youth compared to the labyrinth suggest not only the pattern of their action, a pattern not understood until its completion, but also the pattern of the wanderings, false starts, and errors of the Trojans themselves as they seek Hesperia. The simile looks backwards, to what Aeneas and his men have undergone. Further, the simile itself does not indicate what lies at the heart of the labyrinth; it stresses only the complexity of the maze; its purpose is not mentioned, with the result that it appears incomplete. The Trojan games, too, will be incomplete, for the movements are interrupted by the burning of the ships. This fact reflects on the very wanderings of Aeneas who will not know the significance of his wanderings until they are completed, until he reaches Italy, and especially his father in the underworld. In its immediate context the simile simply describes what is going on, even as Aeneas described to Dido what he had undergone. But in the larger context of books I–VI, the simile suggests that there is more purpose to the pattern than initially appears.[4]

On one other occasion, Vergil cites the Cretan labyrinth in a passage which takes up the allusions just adumbrated. Aeneas views the Daedalian doors leading to the cave of Apollo where the Sibyl presides (VI. 14 ff., esp. 26–30) who will lead him on the path into the underworld. What he sees, in effect, is his own past in symbolic form. The deceitful windings of the labyrinth, and the monstrous result of illicit love that lies at its heart, are analogous to the physical wanderings of Aeneas and the spiritual errors of his own passion for Dido from which he was able to extricate himself only by the thread of divine aid. His past is shown him just as he is about to discover the significance of that mazy past. It is thus to book VI that the simile in book V, applied to the cavalry movements of the Trojan youth, looks forward.

In the very act of playing out these war games, the youth appear like dolphins frisking in the sea. The present appearance of their action is the point of comparison. Despite the seriousness of what they are doing, they do look like creatures at play intent upon their own amusement. The simile lends a lightness to the scene which counteracts some of the ominous tone of the labyrinth simile.

---

[4] Cf. Putnam, pp. 86–87.

Dolphins appear also on the shield of Aeneas, as it is described in book VIII (671–674). The passage occurs between descriptions of civil disturbance: Cato and Catiline on the one hand, on the other the battle of Actium. The similarity of language (*secabant*—VIII. 674, and *secant*—V. 595) recalls the dolphin simile of book V, and anticipates the dolphin simile of book IX where the sea nymphs who were once Aeneas' ships are compared to dolphins:

> et sua quaeque
> continuo puppes abrumpunt vincula ripis
> delphinumque modo demersis aequora rostris
> ima petunt.
>
> (IX.117–120)

Jupiter brings about the change he promised Cybele (IX. 102–103). The fact that Cybele (*Mater Berecyntia*) requested the transformation recalls the simile Anchises had used about Rome and her future children when he was explaining to Aeneas the future greatness of Rome:

> en huius, nate, auspiciis illa incluta Roma
> imperium terris, animos aequabit Olympo,
> septemque una sibi muro circumdabit arces,
> felix prole virum: qualis Berecyntia mater
> invehitur curru Phrygias turrita per urbes
> laeta deum partu, centum complexa nepotes,
> omnis caelicolas, omnis supera alta tenentis.
>
> (VI.781–787)

The simile makes evident that *Roma* is to be like Cybele and rejoice in the protection offered by men. In book X, the sea nymphs who were once ships protect Aeneas and guide his ship safely back to the Trojan camp (219 ff.). The simile of the dolphins forms a link between the Trojan youth and the nymphs so that the activity of the sea nymphs in book X reflects on the boys of book V and indicates that the boys will be like the sea nymphs, for they, too, will eventually protect what Aeneas is to found, and that protection will extend to the future, as the appearance of dolphins on Aeneas' shield hints, as well as Anchises' prophecy tells. The boys are the bulwark of the future; they are the future protection from the dangers of the labyrinth, as the passage of book V (596–603) immediately following the dolphin simile suggests. But it is not until Vergil extrapolates the dolphin simile of V in the subsequent references to dolphins that the full significance of the simile becomes clear.

The next group of similes concerns birds which are in various ways compared to mankind, and implicit throughout the group is the notion of danger. In book V, a simile describes the speeding ship of Mnestheus as a dove in flight:

> qualis spelunca subito commota columba,
> cui domus et dulces latebroso in pumice nidi,
> fertur in arva volans plausumque exterrita pennis
> dat tecto ingentem, mox aëre lapsa quieto
> radit iter liquidum celeris neque commovet alas:
> sic Mnestheus, sic ipsa fuga secat ultima Pristis
> aequora, sic illam fert impetus ipse volantem.
>
> (V.213–219)

This simile is related to one in book II (516) wherein Hecuba and her daughters are compared to terrified doves in a storm, and to one in book IV. The simile of book V expands the brief allusion of book II, where Hecuba and her daughters-in-law are presented as having their home defiled, but as able only to flutter before the onslaught. In book V, the simile describes in greater detail how the dove behaves when suddenly terrified for itself and its nest. But the simile also emphasizes the speed with which Mnestheus' ship moves, testifying to the teamwork of the men aboard it. In a detailed analysis of this passage as part of the illustration of Vergil's subjective style, Otis aptly observes how the reader's feelings for the terror and flight of the dove are transferred to Mnestheus, his ship, and men.[5] But the simile through its allusion to the doves of book II recalls the disaster Hecuba and her daughters-in-law underwent and thereby anticipates the result of this race, for Mnestheus and his men lose to Cloanthus. The boat race is a game where to lose does not cost life, but the description of the contest for one of its players at least has ominous overtones which anticipate ensuing disaster.[6] Doves especially seem to be connected with the idea of a preordained victim, for in a later episode in book V a fluttering dove tied to a mast becomes the target in an archery contest (V. 485–518). The dove first is let loose and then is killed by one man's arrow. However, the dove also presages the omen which Acestes' arrow becomes. Such allusions to the dove suggest not only the destruction of

---

[5] Otis, pp. 59–61.
[6] Putnam, pp. 74 ff. well discusses this point, especially the parallels between Menoetes and Palinurus.

the innocent but also that from the sacrifice something worthwhile emerges, a theme implicit throughout the *Aeneid*. The simile of book V anticipates the result of the race for Mnestheus, and further, the simile and its context anticipate the changed world of the last six books, wherein the world of games is supplanted by the world of reality with life or death as its rewards.

This very point becomes emphatic when it is also remembered that the simile of book V and its context of the boat race recall also a brief simile used of Mercury in book IV, wherein the god is compared to a bird.

> hic primum paribus nitens Cyllenius alis
> constitit; hinc toto praeceps se corpore ad undas
> misit avi similis, quae circum litora, circum
> piscosos scopulos humilis volat aequora iuxta.
>
> (IV.252–255)

The simile stresses the swiftness of Mercury's headlong flight to warn the dallying Aeneas. Mercury, the messenger of the gods, is also the conductor of the dead to the underworld. By comparing Mercury to a bird, Vergil implies that birds may in some way be symbolic of death. In the sequence of bird similes, this simile of Mercury as a bird implies danger and death which may be Aeneas' lot, and so confirms the ominous tone of the similes of the doves used of Hecuba and Mnestheus.

Three more similes involving birds occur in the *Aeneid,* the first in book VII, the second in X, and the third in book XI. The first describes the coming of Messapus' men to swell the army of Latins:

> ceu quondam nivei liquida inter nubila cycni
> cum sese e pastu referunt et longa canoros
> dant per colla modos, sonat amnis et Asia longe
> pulsa palus.
> nec quisquam aeratas acies ex agmine tanto
> misceri putet, aëriam sed gurgite ab alto
> urgeri volucrum raucarum ad litora nubem.
>
> (VII.699–705)

The terms of the simile differ in detail from the previous dove similes. Here swans appear and their noise, not their movement, is the point of comparison. The men singing of their leader (698) are like the swans whose songs re-echo through stream and swamp. The simile effectively makes one aspect of the scene stand for the whole party of men. The men indeed, as the simile tells, do not seem like a bronze

line of battle, but rather a cloud of birds. The simile, one of the three
used in the catalogue of Latin warriors, derives from Homer's simile in
the *Iliad* (II. 459–466), where it is used to suggest the noise of the
entire Greek army. Vergil emphasizes only one body of men who sing
of their leader. As the simile recalls the Greek warriors of the *Iliad,*
and so implies that Messapus' men are comparable to the Danaans of
old, it reinforces a prominent theme of the *Aeneid,* the repetition of
the past: the Trojans are forced to repeat their past, forced to fight a
war comparable to the Trojan war. The motif derives from the hatred
of Juno who will not allow the past to lie buried, and in book VII
Vergil transfers the theme to the society of Latium so that the Latins
become in effect the agents of Juno. Messapus recurs throughout the
last six books of the epic as a doughty warrior whose cries rally the
Latins. Thus the simile looks ahead specifically as well as generally in
its ironic anticipation of the warrior cries of Messapus and his men.
The singing swans become, by the time of book XII, birds of ill-omen,
not only to the Trojans but to the Latins themselves. The swans of
the simile seem also to be connected with the first appearance of swans
in the *Aeneid* (I. 390–400) where Venus interprets the action of the
twelve swans as auguring Aeneas' recovery of a portion of his fleet.

But the simile also anticipates another which compares missiles
to cranes flying across the sky. The crane simile has already been
touched upon[7] and occurs when Aeneas' reappearance heartens the
Trojan camp:

> clamorem ad sidera tollunt
> Dardanidae e muris, spes addita suscitat iras,
> tela manu iaciunt, quales sub nubibus atris
> Strymoniae dant signa grues atque aethera tranant
> cum sonitu, fugiuntque Notos clamore secundo.
>
> (X.262–266)

Even though the simile of the cranes differs somewhat from the previous simile in that the point of the comparison lies in the noise the
weapons as well as the men make, it, nonetheless, like the previous
simile, anticipates the coming attack of the Trojans on the Latins.

Significantly the crane simile of book X also comes from the same
*Iliad* passage as the previous swan simile. Again the reminiscence is of
the Greek army, but now the simile is applied to the weapons of the
Trojans themselves. The weapons by metonymy stand for the men so

---

[7] See p. 34.

that, in effect, the Trojans are comparable to the Greeks who proved victorious at Troy. With the return of Aeneas and his allies, the Trojans will rally to fight against the Latins, and ultimately their cause will prove victorious. The simile, like the return of Aeneas, marks the change in Trojan fortunes.

The bird similes of books II and V differ from those of VII and X. The birds are no longer doves fluttering from fear, but swans and cranes, strong and redoubtable. But the last bird simile to be discussed here reflects, and in a sense recapitulates, the previous similes of this type. It occurs in book XI and compares the clamor of the Latins to that of a flock of birds:

> nuntius ingenti per regia tecta tumultu
> ecce ruit magnisque urbem terroribus implet:
> instructos acie Tiberino a flumine Teucros
> Tyrrhenamque manum totis descendere campis.
> extemplo turbati animi concussaque vulgi
> pectora et arrectae stimulis haud mollibus irae.
> arma manu trepidi poscunt, fremit arma iuventus,
> flent maesti mussantque patres. hic undique clamor
> dissensu vario magnus se tollit in auras:
> haud secus atque alto in luco cum forte catervae
> consedere avium, piscosove amne Padusae
> dant sonitum rauci per stagna loquacia cycni.
>
> (XI.447–458)

The simile occurs after the Latins have listened to Latinus, Drances, and Turnus and have seen with terror the approach of the Trojans. The simile echoes the previous ones, especially that of book VII with its reference to swans. But the import of the simile has changed. The people are no longer joyful in their cries, their bird-like clamor is one of fear. As the previous simile of birds indicated a change in the Trojan fortunes, so this one marks the changed Latin fortunes. This reversal, further, echoes the bird simile of book II where Hecuba and her daughters-in-law fluttered like doves. We have come full circle in these similes and the Latin people are in a position analogous to that of the Trojans in book II. The appearance of the bird similes signifies the varying changes in attitudes of people, changes which resulted from their changed fortunes. At the same time, it is evident that the bird similes by their very repetition of the common motif of birds indicates an underlying unity between the two peoples: Trojans and Latins are basically alike, capable of the same sort of exultation or anxiety. More than any other single group of similes, these bird similes reveal the essential unity of the two peoples—a unity based finally on their common humanity.

Some of the similes drawn from the world of reptiles and animals have a connection with the similes of insects and birds in that they are assimilated to groups of men, but these similes have a more threatening undercurrent than did those of the birds and bees.

The first such simile appears in book II. Laocoon, ensnared by the sea serpents, is described in the following simile:

> ille simul manibus tendit divellere nodos
> perfusus sanie vittas atroque veneno,
> clamores simul horrendos ad sidera tollit:
> qualis mugitus, fugit cum saucius aram
> taurus et incertam excussit cervice securim.
> (II.220–224)

The wounded bull's cry and his attempt to shake the ill-applied ax from his neck form a dramatic and much admired picture of Laocoon. The simile suggests that Laocoon has become the sacrificial victim, taking the place of the bull he had been on the point of sacrificing to Neptune (201–202).[8] Further, it casts light on Laocoon's own passion: he is sacrificed to the sea serpents, to the Greeks, and, finally, to Minerva, the goddess whose agents are the serpents. Laocoon's attempt to deny entrance to the wooden horse causes the attack of the sea monsters, and he is seized in the very act of sacrificing to Neptune. That Laocoon was right in forbidding the Trojans to trust in the horse does not save him, nor does the fact that he is performing a religious rite. Although he represents the worthiness of Troy, Troy itself has lost the protection of the gods, and its people consequently cease to profit from prudent forethought; the Trojans including Aeneas share in willing their own destruction. Laocoon's horrible death confirms the Trojans in accepting the wooden horse, and so with their own hands the Trojans introduce the machine of their own doom. Laocoon, the innocent victim, becomes one of the many prices the Trojans pay for their own blindness.

The entire Laocoon episode elaborates a theme found repeatedly in the *Aeneid*, that from some act in itself bad, good arises. Here Vergil complicates the matter. Laocoon's attempt to save Troy was noble but it caused his own death; hence the good results in evil. But from the

---

[8] Putnam, p. 24.

point of view of the future, Troy could not remain; it had to give
way to the civilization of the west. Hence, in the sacrifice of Laocoon,
the ambiguity of motives and effects which operates throughout the
*Aeneid* becomes particularly evident.[9]

Related to the simile of the wounded bull is another of a wounded
animal. Dido inflamed by her passion for Aeneas is compared to a deer
wounded unwittingly by a hunter:

> uritur infelix Dido totaque vagatur
> urbe furens, qualis coniecta cerva sagitta,
> quam procul incautam nemora inter Cresia fixit
> pastor agens telis liquitque volatile ferrum
> nescius: illa fuga silvas saltusque peragrat
> Dictaeos; haeret lateri letalis harundo.
>
> (IV.68–73)

This simile which will be discussed again later[10] deserves comment at
the moment because it indicates that Dido is like the wounded deer.
Though her own passion is partly responsible for her plight, she is
also the victim of Aeneas. As the simile implies, she will in a sense be
sacrificed for the destiny of Aeneas, for it is through the experience of
this passionate love affair that Aeneas learns how much of his personal
pleasure must be sacrificed for the achievement of his destined mission.
Dido plays a role not unlike Laocoon, nor for that matter unlike
Palinurus.[11]

While these two similes have further ramifications and connections in the similes of books IX–XII, they anticipate an event described in book VII (475–510): Ascanius innocently kills Silvia's pet
deer and so precipitates the war between the Latins and the Trojans.
His act, like his father's in the love affair with Dido, becomes the
unwitting gesture which creates havoc. Silvia's wounded deer is, furthermore, like the sacrifice of Laocoon, an occasion which begins the
conflict between Greeks and Trojans. In all three instances the action
of the Trojans brings about disastrous results: by the two similes Vergil
suggests that innocence can lead to as deadly a result as can malicious
intention, for it is only through action that the potentiality for good
or evil can be realized.

In book II, the book among the first six with the greatest number
of destructive animal similes, the sea monsters which attacked Laocoon

---

[9] Otis, p. 248.
[10] See pp. 91 ff.
[11] On the notion of necessary sacrifice see Putnam, pp. 92–100.

form the basis for two further similes. The first compares the Greek Androgeos, who has happened upon Aeneas' band of Trojans, to a man who has inadvertently stumbled on a snake:

> 'alii rapiunt incensa feruntque
> Pergama: vos celsis nunc primum a navibus itis?'
> dixit, et extemplo (neque enim responsa dabantur
> fida satis) sensit medios delapsus in hostis.
> obstipuit retroque pedem cum voce repressit.
> improvisum aspris veluti qui sentibus anguem
> pressit humi nitens trepidusque repente refugit
> attollentem iras et caerula colla tumentem,
> haud secus Androgeos visu tremefactus abibat.
>
> (II.374–382)

The chiastic arrangement of lines 378–382 emphasizes the serpentine effect of the simile which conveys the horror of what Androgeos has come upon and his sense of entrapment.[12] Like Laocoon, he is encircled by the serpent and destroyed; he becomes a sacrifice. However, the serpents in this simile are not Greeks, but Trojans, and Androgeos is their first victim. By using a simile involving serpents to describe the Trojans, Vergil connects the actions of Aeneas' band with the serpents who destroyed Laocoon, and so the Trojans are like the Greeks who are bent on destroying Troy. The full implication of this point appears immediately, for the band disguises itself as Greek soldiers and is subsequently attacked by fellow Trojans, and in the ensuing melee the greater part of the band is destroyed. In assuming the disguise of the Greeks they have become, as the simile implies, like the sea serpents.

But it is as disguised Greeks that they play this terrifying role, for the Greeks are the real "serpents" bent on enmeshing the city in deadly coils. The next simile of the snake clarifies the point. Pyrrhus enters Priam's palace to kill the old king. As he appears, he is compared to a snake which in springtime sheds its old skin for a new one:

> Vestibulum ante ipsum primoque in limine Pyrrhus
> exsultat telis et luce coruscus aëna:
> qualis ubi in lucem coluber mala gramina pastus,
> frigida sub terra tumidum quem bruma tegebat,
> nunc, positis novus exuviis nitidusque iuventa,
> lubrica convolvit sublato pectore terga
> arduus ad solem, et linguis micat ore trisulcis.
>
> (II.469–475)

---

[12] See pp. 6, 12.

Pyrrhus, as his name implies, is the symbol of the Greek fire destroying the city. Now in the person of Pyrrhus that fire has reached the inner heart of the royal palace. As Pyrrhus bursts into the penetralia, the hidden treachery of the Greeks is fully revealed; the serpents attacking Laocoon are at last understood. Exulting in his strength, Pyrrhus appears like a snake which shed its skin, and in so doing he reveals the might of the Greeks. But the simile also suggests a rebirth, as though Pyrrhus were a renewed Achilles. But just as Pyrrhus is not a snake, so is he not an Achilles, for he lacks, as Priam tells him, the nobility and generosity of his father (540 ff.). Indeed, unlike Achilles, Neoptolemus does not kindly receive the aged king, rather he sends Priam to join his son in Hades. The simile, insofar as it deals with Pyrrhus, suggests in reality that the past has returned with more fiery violence; the Greeks have renewed their vigor. Pyrrhus reincarnates the deadly force of the past at the same time that he fully exposes the hidden imposthume which destroys Troy.

However, we feel as readers that the faint suggestion of a rebirth is nonetheless present in the simile and its context. This feeling comes about because we share the point of view of Aeneas, and that affects our understanding of Aeneas himself. Aeneas had earlier described himself and his band as a coiled serpent. Following the simile in which he sees Pyrrhus as a reborn snake, he speaks of witnessing the devastation of the royal family and of thinking then of his own father and family. It is at this point that Aeneas himself begins to change, to think of something other than his own glory and fame, to shed in fact the old heroic code. For in Priam's fall he witnesses the end of the antique heroism, even though at that point he is not fully conscious of what he sees, nor even is he wholly aware at Dido's court of the significance of what he relates. Nevertheless, it is at that point that the process begins from which Aeneas will emerge, through experience and through instruction, as the new, the civilized, hero. Aeneas had been like Pyrrhus in cruelty and savagery, but when he sees Pyrrhus in action an alteration begins in him; the old skin is sloughed off. Aeneas will not, however, emerge in his new, radiant skin until he dons the divine armor of Vulcan (VIII. 729–731).

A final snake simile appears in book V. Here, however, the simile describes the snake which has been wounded and attempts to recover as best it may. The simile compares the broken ship of Sergestus to a mutilated serpent:

> qualis saepe viae deprensus in aggere serpens,
> aerea quem obliquum rota transiit aut gravis ictu

seminecem liquit saxo lacerumque viator;
nequiquam longos fugiens dat corpore tortus
parte ferox ardensque oculis et sibila colla
arduus attollens; pars vulnere clauda retentat
nexantem nodis seque in sua membra plicantem:
tali remigio navis se tarda movebat;
vela facit tamen et velis subit ostia plenis.

(V.273–281)

It is true that the simile fittingly describes the movement of Sergestus' ship, after he had managed to smash it on the rocks. But the simile recalls the previous similes involving serpents and reminds the reader of what a violent and pervasive role serpents had played in book II. The point of recalling these earlier passages in conjunction with Sergestus' broken ship is to show that the danger symbolized in the serpents is finished, the serpent has been scotched. Sergestus manages to return his maimed ship to the fleet for which he is thanked by Aeneas. The fact that it is Sergestus' ship which was broken may allude to the scotching of Catiline, Sergestus' descendant (cf. V. 121). The change in the serpent similes has been anticipated in book V by the appearance of the snake as symbolic of the spirit of Anchises (84 ff.), a beneficent omen. One other point may also be observed. The serpents which attacked Laocoon came from the sea as did Pyrrhus. Destruction from the sea was closely associated with serpents in the earlier passages. But now that danger is waning and the serpent similes of book V clearly indicate the change. In comparing Sergestus' ship to a maimed serpent, the connection between ships, seas, and serpents becomes evident. But so, too, does the beginning of the end of danger from the sea.[13]

In book II another crucial simile first occurs. Aeneas has just exhorted his band of men to go forth to battle the attacking Greeks:

inde, lupi ceu
raptores atra in nebula, quos improba ventris
exegit caecos rabies catulique relicti
faucibus exspectant siccis, per tela, per hostis
vadimus haud dubiam in mortem mediaeque tenemus
urbis iter; nox atra cava circumvolat umbra.

(II.355–360)

The comparison of the Trojans to wolves aptly fits the rage and desire of the Trojans, and the details of the hunger and thirst for blood of the wolves and their whelps encourages Aeneas' audience to justify

---

[13] Putnam, pp. 80–81.

the behavior of the wolves and so, by implication, the Aeneadae.[14]
But to fight against the Greeks is to defy the instructions of Hector
and to disregard the information of Pantheus, the priest of Apollo.
Despite the seeming justification of his behavior, emphasized in the
simile by . . . *rabies catulique relicti,* Aeneas acts like a madman, as he
earlier claimed:

> exoritur clamorque virum clangorque tubarum.
> arma amens capio; nec sat rationis in armis,
> sed glomerare manum bello et concurrere in arcem
> cum sociis ardent animi; furor iraque mentem
> praecipitat, pulchrumque mori succurrit in armis.
>
> (II.313–317)

Aeneas and his band hunger to save their city and thereby win honor
and glory even if it means death to themselves.[15] Like the wolves they
thirst for blood. But the simile, by alluding to the cubs left behind,
suggests too that the Aeneadae have no business dying and abandoning
the young. The simile and its context indicate that honor and glory
are precisely what they will not find in their mad career. Instead, they
become, as the simile also makes clear, beasts marauding in their
own city. The simile occurs at the beginning of the episode in which
Aeneas' band, after donning Greek armor, is eventually destroyed. The
disguise of Greek armor is comparable then to the wolves prowling in
the dark shadows of the night: both groups are hidden. The simile
forms a prelude to that encounter and to the snake simile, already discussed, and it anticipates the folly of the Aeneadae. Significantly, it
occurs at the lowest point in Aeneas' moral history, for on only one
other occasion in the *Aeneid* is Aeneas compared to an animal.[16]

The next wolf simile does not occur until book IX where Turnus
rages against the besieged Trojans:

> ac veluti pleno lupus insidiatus ovili
> cum fremit ad caulas ventos perpessus et imbris
> nocte super media; tuti sub matribus agni
> balatum exercent, ille asper et improbus ira
> saevit in absentis; collecta fatigat edendi
> ex longo rabies et siccae sanguine fauces:
> haud aliter Rutulo muros et castra tuenti
> ignescunt irae, duris dolor ossibus ardet.
>
> (IX.59–66)

---

[14] See also pp. 9, 92.
[15] See also pp. 13 ff., 22 ff., 31, 36, 91, 101.
[16] In book XII, see pp. 132 ff. and 134 ff.

The details of the simile deliberately recall the simile of book II: Turnus is a wolf driven on by hunger to ravage a sheepfold at night.[17] The Trojans are safe enough so long as they keep to their camp, even as the sheep before the threat of the marauding wolf. The hunger which drives Turnus is the hunger for slaughter of his enemies and for fame, even as had been the case with the Trojan band. The simile calls up pathos for the Trojans who are compared to sheep, and at the same time it reduces Turnus to the level of a violent animal. But even so, there are differences to be observed between men and animals. In a sense what the wolf does in pursuing the sheep is a natural action, but what Turnus does is not; the appearance of the two patterns of behavior is the same, but the motivation of each differs. It is in this discrepancy that the horror and pathos of the simile ultimately lie. The simile is the first of many in the last six books which explores these motifs and defines the moral ambiguity of the various actions. Because it deliberately recalls the wolf simile used of Aeneas and his band of Trojans, the simile serves to foreshadow Turnus' own destruction. For as Aeneas and the Trojans were finally unsuccessful against the Greeks at Troy, so ultimately will Turnus be against Aeneas.

The moral ambiguity implicit in similes of animals is not limited to Latins, for in the next such simile Trojans are involved. Euryalus is compared to a hungry lion around a sheep pen:[18]

> impastus ceu plena leo per ovilia turbans
> (suadet enim vesana fames) manditque trahitque
> molle pecus mutumque metu, fremit ore cruento:
> nec minor Euryali caedes; incensus et ipse
> perfurit ac multam in medio sine nomine plebem,
> Fadumque Herbesumque subit Rhoetumque Abarimque
> ignaros; Rhoetum vigilantem et cuncta videntem,
> sed magnum metuens se post cratera tegebat.
>
> (IX.339–346)

Nisus and Euryalus at this point have left the Trojan camp to inform Aeneas of the danger facing the Trojans, and on their way they slaughter a number of the sleeping Latin soldiers. The entire Nisus and Euryalus episode is a fascinating exploration of moral ambiguity. The two youths, hungry for fame as warriors, deliberately disobey Aeneas' command to remain in camp until he returns. In the simile and its context, hunger for the first time is explicitly equated not only

---

[17] See also pp. 9 ff.
[18] See also pp. 10, 71, 120.

with slaughter but with spoils and glory. They go forth, emboldened
by the promise of great rewards from Ascanius and high praise from
the Trojans. The leaders themselves are also culpable, for they want
to send a messenger to Aeneas (IX. 226–228), but Aeneas' orders were
that no one should leave the camp (IX. 41–42). That the Trojan
leaders deliberate about sending a message to him, and acquiesce in
Nisus' scheme, suggests that they regard disobeying a general's orders
as a light matter. But Nisus and Euryalus further complicate their
disobedience by slaughtering the Latins, and because of Euryalus'
greed for booty, they are found and destroyed by a party of Latins.
The onus of their destruction falls upon Euryalus' passion for fame
and Nisus' passion for his friend. While describing their exploit and
death in moving terms, Vergil nevertheless wants his readers to observe
the ambiguity of their motives and their terrible irresponsibility. In
the simile used to compare Euryalus to a lion, Vergil indicates how the
hunger for fame and glory reduces its victim to the level of an animal
—unthinking and unreasoning, and it is in the simile that we perceive
the moral indictment Vergil makes on the two youths. Yet he could
not have done so had he not prepared the way for this lion simile with
its repetition of the motif of hunger by his previous similes involving
a wolf. The simile in its details recapitulates and at the same time
expands on the previous animal similes. The rage of Turnus like
the rage of Aeneas in book II becomes, then, comparable to the rage
of Nisus and Euryalus—a rage for glory and destruction, a rage of
maddened beasts thirsting for blood.

The next animal simile in book IX changes the emphasis, for
here Helenor, a Trojan, is compared to a beast trapped by hunters,
but an animal who nonetheless rushes against his captors in a vain
attempt to escape:

> isque ubi se Turni media inter milia vidit,
> hinc acies atque hinc acies astare Latinas,
> ut fera, quae densa venantum saepta corona
> contra tela furit seseque haud nescia morti
> inicit et saltu supra venabula fertur—
> haud aliter iuvenis medios moriturus in hostis
> inruit et qua tela videt densissima tendit.
>
> (IX.549–555)

The Trojan has become the hunted animal, not unlike Dido, the
hunted doe of book IV. But Helenor rushes headlong to his doom,
failing to follow the path of prudence. The simile's description echoes

the death of Euryalus who was also surrounded and trapped by hunters and who died not unlike a beast at bay, so that the death of Helenor, a young man, echoes the death of the other youth.

The very next simile carries on this allusion to the death of Nisus and Euryalus. Lycus, a friend of Helenor but swifter of foot, is almost safely home when he is captured and destroyed by Turnus:

> at pedibus longe melior Lycus inter et hostis
> inter et arma fuga muros tenet, altaque certat
> prendere tecta manu sociumque attingere dextras.
> quem Turnus pariter cursu teloque secutus
> increpat his victor: 'nostrasne evadere, demens,
> sperasti te posse manus?' simul arripit ipsum
> pendentem et magna muri cum parte revellit:
> qualis ubi aut leporem aut candenti corpore cycnum
> sustulit alta petens pedibus Iovis armiger uncis,
> quaesitum aut matri multis balatibus agnum
> Martius a stabulis rapuit lupus.
>
> (IX.556–566)

The simile expands on earlier ones in that it picks up the allusion of Turnus to a wolf, but adds the reference to an eagle. Lycus is compared to a rabbit or a swan or (and most crucially) a lamb. We see Turnus as the predatory creature, even as the wolf of the earlier simile, triumphant over a helpless creature.

But more can be said about these two similes. Helenor and Lycus both fall like Nisus and Euryalus. They are like animals at bay, even as the Trojans were before the Greeks at Troy. Both similes, further, emphasize the death of the two young Trojans and both extrapolate on Turnus as marauding beast. At the same time, particularly in the Lycus simile, another creature is added—the eagle who seizes in its talons helpless creatures, a point Vergil will use in later similes. The phrase *Iovis armiger uncis* for the eagle of Jupiter deserves comment. It recalls the rape of Ganymede (cf. V. 250–255 and I. 28), one of the causes contributing to Juno's endless hostility to the Trojans. Juno through her champion, Turnus, in effect revenges herself for the rape of Ganymede by the destruction of the Trojan youth Lycus. Turnus' action is one in a long series which keeps alive past enmity. No possibility of the future can exist until that enmity is allayed. The simile, like the event it describes, effectively marks the constancy of the deadly past in the present. Finally, in the Lycus simile, by the way in which Lycus dies—Turnus destroys Lycus and in so doing pulls down part of a defensive wall—the point is made clear that the men are the wall;

they are the defensive rampart of the Trojan camp. In his destruction of the man and the wall, Turnus repeats a similar action of the Aeneadae of book II who pulled down a tower which thereupon crashed over the Grecian ranks:

> turrim in praecipiti stantem summisque sub astra
> eductam tectis, unde omnis Troia videri
> et Danaum solitae naves et Achaica castra,
> adgressi ferro circum, qua summa labantis
> iuncturas tabulata dabant, convellimus altis
> sedibus impulimusque; ea lapsa repente ruinam
> cum sonitu trahit et Danaum super agmina late
> incidit.
>
> (II.460–467)

Two more similes of book IX emphasize Turnus as ravaging beast attacking defenseless herds. Pandarus, the Trojan, at last shuts the gates he and his brother Bitias had foolishly opened, and in doing so he inadvertently locks Turnus within the camp, a tiger within the pen:[19]

> ast alios secum includit recipitque ruentis,
> demens, qui Rutulum in medio non agmine regem
> viderit inrumpentem ultroque incluserit urbi,
> immanem veluti pecora inter inertia tigrim.
>
> (IX.727–730)

The Trojans are again compared to helpless creatures before the attack of a more powerful beast. Turnus as ravening monster recapitulates what we have already seen of him.

But even the animal, fierce as a lion, can at last be turned, and this is what happens to Turnus within the Trojan camp. He is compared to a lion pressed by a throng of men with savage weapons:

> acrius hoc Teucri clamore incumbere magno
> et glomerare manum, ceu saevum turba leonem
> cum telis premit infensis; at territus ille,
> asper, acerba tuens, retro redit et neque terga
> ira dare aut virtus patitur, nec tendere contra
> ille quidem hoc cupiens potis est per tela virosque.
> haud aliter retro dubius vestigia Turnus
> improperata refert et mens exaestuat ira.
>
> (IX.791–798)

---

[19] See also p. 11.

Turnus, at this point, escapes, but not before he is almost destroyed.[20] The use of the lion and the tiger as the vehicle for a simile calls to mind Euryalus who was similarly compared, and, in the light of what happened to that youth, the simile implies that a like fate ultimately awaits Turnus.

The similes of book IX derive from the wolf simile of book II. They repeatedly emphasize Turnus as a powerful, wild animal, and the Trojans as defenseless and usually helpless creatures, like lambs or herds. The Trojans are at this point without their leader, their shepherd, and so before the onslaught of the Latin forces react in a manner comparable to docile flocks. The similes, in addition, emphasize the fact that war reduces the men on both sides to animals who are unthinking creatures. Yet the similes imply that animals, even dangerous beasts, can eventually be overcome by men. The similes reflect not only the action of book IX, but they also illuminate the moral judgments Vergil wants observed. Both Latins and Trojans in the course of the action of the book act irresponsibly: both sides are guilty of foolhardy actions entailing destruction for their own men. The Trojans, in disobeying Aeneas' command to remain within the camp, react to the attack of the Latin forces like unthinking animals; they are brave and to a great degree fearless, but ultimately they fail to perceive the consequences of their activity. What they fail to realize is their essentially weak position because they lack the foresight of their leader. The Latins, as well, suffer destruction, but they do so precisely because of their leader. Turnus is finally senseless of all things except his own glory, indifferent to everything but the satisfaction of his own hunger. He does not think to open the gates of the Trojan camp and so end the war; because of his indifference to all but himself, he is like the lone animal who relies on his own brute force to carry all before him. While his great glory rests in his rage, that rage will cause his ultimate defeat and that of the Latin forces. Book IX implies emphatically through its accumulation of animal similes that men are finally superior to beasts. When men fail to comprehend their distinction, they aid in their own destruction. No other book in the *Aeneid* explores as fully as book IX does the moral ambivalence in comparing men and animals.

Book X continues the war between Trojans and Latins, and in it three animal similes compare two Latin chieftains. The first observes the approach of Turnus upon Pallas as a lion springing upon a bull:

---

[20] See also pp. 11, 120.

> desiluit Turnus biiugis, pedes apparat ire
> comminus; utque leo, specula cum vidit ab alta
> stare procul campis meditantem in proelia taurum,
> advolat: haud alia est Turni venientis imago.
>
> (X.453–456)

The emphasis of the simile lies in the suddenness of the movement. The animals are both strong, as befits Turnus and Pallas. Yet because of its ability to move swiftly and unexpectedly, the lion clearly has the advantage over the bull, as the epithet for the latter implies (*meditantem*). The simile hints at the approaching death of Pallas. Pallas, like a bull just as Laocoon in book II, is about to be offered up as sacrifice to Turnus' rage, even as the bullock died in book V (477–481) in place of Dares. But the fact that Turnus is compared to a lion recalls the lion similes of Euryalus and Turnus in book IX and their connotations of unthinking rage for blood and fame. Turnus in his ardent pursuit of Pallas gives way to a blind rage for fame, a rage which will continue through his unmerciful destruction of the younger man, and will die at last as a consequence of his brutal slaying and despoiling of Pallas. The simile of the lion attacking the bull looks forward not only to the death of Pallas, but by its association with the simile of Euryalus to that of Turnus as well.

Through the agency of Juno, Turnus is driven for his own sake from the field of battle and his place is taken by Mezentius. Mezentius serves as a "double" for the Latin leader, and two animal similes bring out this "doublet" aspect of Mezentius. The first describes Mezentius as a boar which, although attacked by men and dogs, nevertheless retains an awesome aspect:

> ac velut ille canum morsu de montibus altis
> actus aper, multos Vesulus quem pinifer annos
> defendit multosque palus Laurentia, silva
> pastus harundinea, postquam inter retia ventum est,
> substitit infremuitque ferox et inhorruit armos,
> nec cuiquam irasci propiusque accedere virtus,
> sed iaculis tutisque procul clamoribus instant;
> ille autem impavidus partis cunctatur in omnis
> dentibus infrendens et tergo decutit hastas:
> haud aliter, iustae quibus est Mezentius irae,
> non ulli est animus stricto concurrere ferro,
> missilibus longe et vasto clamore lacessunt.
>
> (X.707–718)

Mezentius comes into the thick of the fighting, and though he is caught there, none of the Trojans is able to overcome him. The simile, in showing Mezentius as a boar at bay, recalls the lion at bay simile used of Turnus at the end of book IX.

The next simile compares Mezentius to a hunger-maddened lion:

> impastus stabula alta leo ceu saepe peragrans
> (suadet enim vesana fames), si forte fugacem
> conspexit capream aut surgentem in cornua cervum,
> gaudet hians immane comasque arrexit et haeret
> visceribus super incumbens; lavit improba taeter
> ora cruor—
> sic ruit in densos alacer Mezentius hostis.
>
> (X.723–729)

The comparison to a lion points up still more strongly Mezentius' role as a double for Turnus; it echoes the lion simile used of Euryalus in book IX (339–346) as well as the tiger and lion similes used of Turnus in that book. The brutal picture of the lion's mouth dripping blood conveys the ultimate savagery and bestiality of the lust for glory in war.

The two similes taken together presage, first, the bringing to bay of a still dangerous enemy, Turnus, and perhaps, more broadly, of all the enemies of civilization, the brutish hungerers after the spoils of war; and secondly, in the subsequent defeat of Mezentius at the hands of Aeneas, the only warrior able to overthrow him, the final defeat of Turnus himself by Aeneas.

The animal similes of book X continue to explore the motifs and themes found in the similes of book IX. But in book XI a change occurs in these similes, for the animals are not the savage beasts of the two earlier books. Although they frequently are rapacious, their savagery is not so forcefully stressed. The first animal simile of book XI describes Turnus after the council of the Latins and at the approach of the Trojans as a frisky horse:

> iamque adeo rutilum thoraca indutus aënis
> horrebat squamis surasque incluserat auro,
> tempora nudus adhuc, laterique accinxerat ensem,
> fulgebatque alta decurrens aureus arce
> exsultatque animis et spe iam praecipit hostem:
> qualis ubi abruptis fugit praesepia vinclis
> tandem liber equus, campoque potitus aperto
> aut ille in pastus armentaque tendit equarum
> aut adsuetus aquae perfundi flumine noto
> emicat, arrectisque fremit cervicibus alte
> luxurians luduntque iubae per colla, per armos.
>
> (XI.487–497)

The simile conveys none of the destructiveness of the earlier animal similes. Indeed, it comes almost as a respite after them. Yet in its context the simile defines an animal-like characteristic of Turnus. He gambols and exults, rejoicing in his strength as he girds for war, for he is at last released from the confinement of the council. In his eyes, he has no need of bridle or rein; he has after all, as his previous speech has indicated, his own strength. The simile stresses just this point, the riderless horse confident in itself. But by stressing that point the simile has a dark undertone, for reliance on strength alone leads to death. The simile is also a reminder, although in a minor key, of a recurrent theme in the *Aeneid:* the perilous loosing of ungovernable·and treacherous forces; for example, the winds in book I which were let loose to rage, the loosing of Sinon by Priam, and most importantly for this passage, the unloosening of the burden of the Trojan Horse. In this simile, the horse has broken its own bonds and has become a law unto itself, pursuing solely its own delights. Remembering the events which precede the simile, we are aware that this unbridled freedom has been seized against counsel. Here then is suggested the lawlessness, even perhaps the *furor,* which it is the task of civilization to curb and enchain, as Jupiter once told Venus (I. 291–296).[21]

Two more similes in book XI convey the rapaciousness of the natural world. Both involve birds, specifically a hawk and an eagle which fly off with small prey. The two similes are companion pieces and describe both Camilla and Tarchon. The first occurs after Camilla has just defeated Ligus:

> 'vane Ligus frustraque animis elate superbis,
> nequiquam patrias temptasti lubricus artis,
> nec fraus te incolumem fallaci perferet Auno.'
> haec fatur virgo, et pernicibus ignea plantis
> transit equum cursu frenisque adversa prehensis
> congreditur poenasque inimico ex sanguine sumit:
> quam facile accipiter saxo sacer ales ab alto
> consequitur pennis sublimem in nube columbam
> comprensamque tenet pedibusque eviscerat uncis;
> tum cruor et vulsae labuntur ab aethere plumae.
>                                        (XI.715–724)

In an effortless fashion, the hawk with its talons, Camilla, overcomes and rends the dove, Ligus. The simile recalls the other bird similes of the poem where the emphasis had been on the more peaceful or

---

[21] Putnam, pp. 3–63, and also consult the index in Otis for page references.

defenseless qualities of the birds. But here the bird becomes a bird of prey, not unlike the eagle and the wolf in the similes of Turnus in book IX. But what makes this particular simile so horrifying and so effective is that the bird of prey represents Camilla. She has reversed nature in her own life to become the unfeminine creature she is. So, too, in the simile the bird of prey pursues the weaker creature of its own species.

The companion simile redresses the imbalance in comparing Tarchon, the ally of the Trojans, to an eagle flying off with a captured snake:

> utque volans alte raptum cum fulva draconem
> fert aquila implicuitque pedes atque unguibus haesit,
> saucius at serpens sinuosa volumina versat
> arrectisque horret squamis et sibilat ore
> arduus insurgens, illa haud minus urget obunco
> luctantem rostro, simul aethera verberat alis:
> haud aliter praedam Tiburtum ex agmine Tarchon
> portat ovans.
>
> (XI.751–758)

By contrast with the previous simile, this one places greater emphasis on the writhing snake; Tarchon exults like the soaring eagle in his prey. The simile not only involves a bird of destruction but also a serpent, and it is here that the hostility associated in book II with the serpent is at last ended, for Tarchon, as a type of Aeneas, triumphs over the snake.

Both Camilla and Tarchon as hawk and eagle deserve comment. Tarchon, whose ancestry descends from Jupiter, merits the comparison, for the eagle is the bird sacred to the ruler of Olympus. Camilla, on the other hand, is called in the terms of the simile a *sacer ales*. The use of a masculine phrase to describe her underscores her own masculinity while the epithet *sacer* reminds us that Camilla, the devotee of Diana, is in her own right *sacer,* as her death will soon make clear. Fittingly, she is compared to a hawk, the bird sacred to Apollo, Diana's brother, for the comparison thereby conveys Camilla's masculinity and her sacredness. But Camilla is *sacer* also in the sense of accursed, for she has perverted her own nature. The actions of both Camilla and Tarchon earn for them the comparison to mighty birds, yet at the same time such a comparison recalls the dominant theme of these similes, namely that war reduces the combatants to something less than human.

The next simile, the last of book XI, reinforces this point. Arruns, having killed Camilla, slinks off the field, and is described as a wolf who has killed a shepherd and hides after the deed:

> ac velut ille, prius quam tela inimica sequantur,
> continuo in montis sese avius abdidit altos
> occiso pastore lupus magnove iuvenco,
> conscius audacis facti, caudamque remulcens
> subiecit pavitantem utero silvasque petivit:
> haud secus ex oculis se turbidus abstulit Arruns
> contentusque fuga mediis se immiscuit armis.
>
> (XI.809–815)

By killing Camilla, Arruns is like the wolf conscious of his boldness; nevertheless, unlike the wolf Arruns will be forced to take responsibility for his act, since Diana will soon see to it that Arruns is killed. In slinking away like a wolf, Arruns echoes the pattern of behavior of the Trojans and Aeneas after their encounter with the overwhelming force of Greeks in book II.

In the simile, Camilla is compared to a shepherd or to a great bullock. Both emphasize again her masculinity. Moreover, in likening her to a shepherd, the simile ironically comments on Camilla: she has led her forces in a wicked cause and, before she can aid them, she herself is struck down so that ultimately she is powerless. She is also like the bullock in being sacrificed, for Camilla like the other Latin heroes is a type for Turnus. The sacrifice of a bullock for a man occurred in book V; here the terms are reversed. Her death is a sacrifice for Turnus, even as Mezentius' was, for in dying she postpones for a while Turnus' own death. But her death like that of all the other heroes, both Trojan and Latin, is a sacrifice demanded of the new civilization Aeneas bears. The heroic code under which all of these heroic creatures function must yield to a civilized life in which the selfish ends of the individual are suppressed or transformed into the new community. Arruns and Camilla both are sacrificed; Arruns to the past, though in a small way he makes the future possible; Camilla to the future, for she is representative of the unusable past. That book XI should end with such a simile emphasizes the pathos Vergil wants to show at these deaths.

The similes involving animals, whether insects, birds, or beasts, show a marked distinction between the first and second halves of the *Aeneid*. Books I–VI, in general, explore through these similes the hope of a natural, harmonious world, a world denied Aeneas who is cast in the role of a wanderer and at the same time a learner. In books

VII–XI, the similes suggest and derive from the world of warfare where men are reduced to predatory beasts, searching not for harmony, for the life lived in accord with nature, but life lived in terms of one's own aggrandisement. This theme appears in book II in the ravaging of Troy by both Greeks and Trojans. Even Aeneas himself appears as something like an animal, a comparison that occurs at the lowest ebb of Aeneas' own fortunes, when he becomes an enemy to his own city. But because of his education Aeneas emerges as the hero who transcends the ancient heroic code. The reduction of the unthinking Latins and Trojans in the books VII–XI to animals, significantly enough, never involves Aeneas.

In books I–VI, with the exception of book II, the use of these similes suggests repeatedly that human beings are like defenseless animals preyed upon by stronger creatures, despite their yearning to live in terms of an harmonious ordering of life. In books VII–XI, however, the similes are used predominantly to explore the notion of people preying on others. They prey for the sake of glory, for fame. But in each instance where such a notion occurs, it results in destruction. Vergil shows that the rage for fame is a deadly and destructive rage involving not only victims, but victors alike. To neither is there any salvation.

The reason he is able to do so, to show the deadly effects of this sort of behavior, arises from the irony implicit in these similes, that men are finally not comparable to animals. There exists a wide gap between the two, even as there existed a gap between the tenor and vehicle of the similes of destructive nature discussed in the previous chapter. Unlike animals, men are capable of reason and so of foresight. They need not be bound by the demands of self-protection nor by the overwhelming demands for the satisfaction of their own lustful desires. At the same time, men are held accountable for their actions; through their very ability to talk and to reason they become responsible agents. The similes derive much of their effectiveness and all of their moral commentary from the difference. This point extends even to the seemingly innocent and passive victims who figure repeatedly in the similes. The reduction of the attacked victims, as book IX shows, to the level of herds and beasts *en masse* implies that they could have been other than they were. Even victims—when they are human beings—could have escaped the devastation which they almost willingly bring on themselves. They do not think, they do not respond as sentient men, and therefore they are like animals who pathetically are attacked and destroyed.

A further point derived from those already mentioned is that of the sacrificial victim. Repeatedly men or animals are sacrificed for the sake of either the past or the future. Book V brings this point out with great clarity. Yet in the later books men are sacrificed much as animals once were. In the sacrifice of men lies the tragedy of so many of the deaths which occur in books IX–XI. For one of the great points the *Aeneid* makes is the folly, the ultimate frivolity of such deaths. Through the similes Vergil conveys the full horror of what war, particularly civil war, demands in the way of sacrifice. For that reason he involves both Trojans and Latins in these animal similes; both are profoundly culpable, for they will not learn, will not profit. Man's first responsibility, and his ultimate one, is to himself as an aware being. Failure to live in accord with that imperative reduces him to the level of the animal, effectively destroys society—even the society man thinks he protects—and finally denies him access to the divine. Dido and Turnus are the classic exemplars of the failure to perceive this truth, and both destroy themselves and injure their fellows. The divinity which they appeal to, exemplified by Juno, must abandon them. But Aeneas, who starts his career in darkness and rage, becomes the paradigm of the man who learns to know himself and to live in accord with that knowledge, and it is his mission to lead his people to peace, to the acceptance of something other than the role of brutes in the organization of society.

In the animal similes of the *Aeneid*, perhaps, can be seen yet another bit of evidence of how Vergil transformed the epic tradition.[22] For example, as has already been noted, Vergil employs similes which derive from Homer. But Homer's animal similes did not form the kind of patterns which we have been observing in Vergil's *Aeneid*. They were, as has been said, of single significance, emphasizing a single point of comparison. Particularly does this seem to be so of the animal similes wherein the point of the comparison is usually speed, prowess, or some other such notion.[23] Vergil, of course, does the same thing; it was, after all, part of the tradition, and he wrote for an audience whose ancestors traced their origin back to the heroic world. But Vergil was also at pains to show how that heroic code needed to be changed and adapted to the demands as well as the needs of civilized society, particularly the society Augustus hoped would emerge from his rule. Therefore, Vergil employs in his similes motifs similar to

[22] Otis, pp. 5–40.
[23] See pp. 6 ff. and the references cited there.

those of Homer, but by his variations on and transformation of a repeated basic motif he multiplies the angles of vision upon a given subject and so draws from the reader not only a more complex emotional response but also judgment. Thus, in repeatedly comparing Turnus to a lion, for instance, he elicits from us, not only sequentially but simultaneously, admiration for the warrior's undeniably superb courage and strength, regret that so brave a man should die untimely, and the recognition that his great qualities have been misdirected, ill-used, and are finally destructive. He exploits the simile in the way neither Homer nor Apollonius ever did.

*Chapter 3*

# Nature:

# Trees and Flowers

Among the similes of the *Aeneid,* a small, interconnected group compares men to trees or flowers. Although the majority occur in the first
six books of the epic, all of them are related to the first in book II, and
it is from the powerful presentation of that simile that the force of the
subsequent ones partly derives. It occurs immediately after Aeneas has
seen, through his mother's aid, the gods dismantling Troy. He recognizes the utter hopelessness of attempting to save Troy:

> Tum vero omne mihi visum considere in ignis
> Ilium et ex imo verti Neptunia Troia;
> ac veluti summis antiquam in montibus ornum
> cum ferro accisam crebrisque bipennibus instant
> eruere agricolae certatim, illa usque minatur
> et tremefacta comam concusso vertice nutat,
> vulneribus donec paulatim evicta supremum
> congemuit traxitque iugis avulsa ruinam.
>
> (II.624–631)

The gods, like the farmers in the simile, strike with repeated ax-blows
the ancient ash tree which is Troy, until at last they succeed in toppling it. The tree takes on a human personality through the personification implicit in such words and phrases as *tremefacta comam,
concusso vertice nutat, vulneribus,* and *congemuit.* Furthermore, the
passage recalls Priam's mutilated corpse which was seen by Aeneas as
an *ingens truncus,* literally a vast tree trunk (II. 557). The pathos

elicited for the tree through the use of personification is transferred then to Troy itself. When the city falls it crashes like the ash tree, bringing utter ruin in its wake. The agents of destruction for the city are the gods, and for the tree, farmers. The work in both cases is a strenuous one, but one which eventually prevails. The tree is seen from a distance, just as Troy is seen through the fire and smoke, so that although Aeneas knows what is happening, i.e., the gods are destroying the city, the event appears eerie and mysterious. And indeed it is, for the fall of a city, like the fall of a tree, changes the landscape before us, and so an aspect of the world.

The next simile, the only epic one of book III, compares the Cyclopes to trees:

> cernimus astantis nequiquam lumine torvo
> Aetnaeos fratres caelo capita alta ferentis,
> concilium horrendum: quales cum vertice celso
> aëriae quercus aut coniferae cyparissi
> constiterunt, silva alta Iovis lucusve Dianae.
> (III.677–681)

To Aeneas and his men, the shaggy and fierce Cyclopes who have one eye, says Achaemenides, equal in size to an Argolic shield or even to the sun (637), appear like giant oaks or cypresses. Though the point of the comparison lies in the Cyclopes' size and shagginess, the simile nevertheless conveys a notion of their awesome strength which could be dangerous to whomsoever the Cyclopes' gaze falls. But if their eye is blinded, they are rendered partially helpless. The terms of this simile are like those of the earlier one, but now trees are used to convey the appearance and strength not of a city, but of men, specifically half-human, half-divine. The simile stresses the immobility of the Cyclopes and their inability to harm Aeneas if he keeps moving. The awesomeness of the previous simile is retained but in a modified fashion, for the reference to the sacred groves of Jupiter and Diana conveys the same mysterious effect which distance lent to the ash tree simile of Troy.

The comparison of the Cyclopes to trees serves as a halfway point between the first of the tree similes and the third, which describes Aeneas as an oak before the storm of Anna's pleas:

> Talibus orabat, talisque miserrima fletus
> fertque refertque soror. sed nullis ille movetur
> fletibus aut voces ullas tractabilis audit;

fata obstant placidasque viri deus obstruit auris.
ac velut annoso validam cum robore quercum
Alpini Boreae nunc hinc nunc flatibus illinc
eruere inter se certant; it stridor, et altae
consternunt terram concusso stipite frondes;
ipsa haeret scopulis et quantum vertice ad auras
aetherias, tantum radice in Tartara tendit:
haud secus adsiduis hinc atque hinc vocibus heros
tunditur, et magno persentit pectore curas;
mens immota manet, lacrimae volvuntur inanes.

(IV.437–449)

This simile has been discussed before in connection with the storm similes,[1] but as part also of the tree similes it deserves further notice. Aeneas remains firm before the onslaught, just as a deeply-rooted oak (the sacred tree of Jupiter, as the Cyclopes simile showed) remains firm. Unlike Troy, it is not the concerted attack of men Aeneas here has to withstand, but something no more grave in import than the buffeting of a northern Alpine gale. Aeneas' presentation as a tree sacred to Jupiter also suggests that at this point the gods are on his side, but there is no assurance that Aeneas' stamina alone can yet withstand any or all disasters.

The fourth simile of a tree compares Entellus, repeatedly struck by Dares in the boxing match, to a hollow pine tree:

Entellus viris in ventum effudit et ultro
ipse gravis graviterque ad terram pondere vasto
concidit, ut quondam cava concidit aut Erymantho
aut Ida in magna radicibus eruta pinus.

(V.446–449)

Entellus falls before Dares' blows and appears to the watching Trojans like the hollow pine tree overturned, roots and all. The simile again compares a man to a tree, but this time the tree is a hollow one, a dead one capable of toppling over at the slightest blow. Thus, it is unlike the previous trees which were firmly rooted and living things deriving sustenance from the earth itself. The simile stresses only the appearance of Entellus, not his inward stamina. For as the upshot of the boxing match proves, Entellus gathers his strength together, is helped up, and goes on to defeat Dares. The simile, therefore, acquires an ironic quality, for the appearance of Entellus belies his reality. A new note

---

[1] See pp. 26 ff.

has been added to the tree simile, for previously both the man and the tree were strong. But Vergil stresses the disparity between appearance and reality, because he wants to emphasize the inner firmness of Entellus as well as his recovery. The notion of firmness of purpose appeared also in the oak simile of book IV, for there too it was Aeneas' firmness of purpose which like the oak prevailed. Vergil expands the significance of the tree in these last two similes in that they concern not just the outward appearance of men, but their inner core, their own character.

The last simile comparing men to trees occurs in book IX. Emboldened by Ascanius' recent success in killing one of the Latin warriors attacking the camp, Pandarus and Bitias, youths from the region of Ida sacred to Jupiter and the Magna Mater, have just opened the gates of the Trojan camp, in defiance of Aeneas' orders. Pandarus and Bitias are ironically compared to twin oaks:

> ipsi intus dextra ac laeva pro turribus astant
> armati ferro et cristis capita alta corusci:
> quales aëriae liquentia flumina circum
> sive Padi ripis Athesim seu propter amoenum
> consurgunt geminae quercus intonsaque caelo
> attollunt capita et sublimi vertice nutant.
> (IX.677–682)

The simile again makes clear how their mighty appearance is like that of lofty oak trees. It is this notion of appearance that the simile like that of Entellus stresses. But, in the light of what happens, their appearance belies the reality, as in the boxing episode. This time the oak trees appear strong, not hollow and capable of being toppled. Yet the event proves Pandarus and Bitias are hollow men. First, they had no business opening the gates to the Latin army. Next, they themselves are not strong enough to withstand the attack of Turnus and his men, for both brothers are killed. They do not emerge as valiant oaks, firmly rooted as is Aeneas, and so their destruction comes about because of their own foolhardiness. The simile occurs at the very start of the scene and serves as an ironic commentary on what ensues. The brothers too are felled even as was the city of Troy. Indeed, Bitias' fall by a *phalarica*, whose power is like a thunderbolt's (705), is fittingly compared to the fall of masonry (710 ff.), and so also does Pandarus' death suggest, through the language used, the fall of a city (752 ff.).

Through the series of tree similes we have come full circle. As Troy involved men and was compared to a tree, now men who have been compared to trees die in the fashion of the falling city. Through these similes, Vergil explores the ambiguity of comparing cities and men to trees, to suggest that the man or city, like a tree, can stand firm only when deeply rooted and firmly fixed, only when appearance mirrors the reality of the inward character.

Related to these similes of trees are two others, both in book VI, one of which concerns mistletoe and the other the leaves of a tree. The simile of mistletoe is used to compare the golden bough Aeneas finds in the sacred wood, before he sets out on his journey through the underworld:

> inde ubi venere ad fauces grave olentis Averni,
> tollunt se celeres liquidumque per aëra lapsae
> sedibus optatis geminae super arbore sidunt,
> discolor unde auri per ramos aura refulsit.
> quale solet silvis brumali frigore viscum
> fronde virere nova, quod non sua seminat arbos,
> et croceo fetu teretis circumdare truncos,
> talis erat species auri frondentis opaca
> ilice, sic leni crepitabat brattea vento.
>
> (VI.201–209)

At first notice the comparison of the golden bough to mistletoe seems odd, and, indeed, commentators from the time of Servius have been puzzled by the simile.[2] The point of the simile lies in the fact that the dark green foliage of the mistletoe, in the depths of winter, suggests life in the midst of death. In one sense the bough is a symbol of life; but in another sense the bough is a symbol for death, since it is not a real plant but a magical growth with metal leaves. The connection between the bough and mistletoe becomes clearer if the passage in its context is scrutinized.

Aeneas is led by the doves of his mother to discover the golden bough in the dark wood. The doves lead him *ad fauces grave olentis Averni* which the dark wood borders on, and there on a tree appears the golden bough. The fact that the bough is hidden implies the need of help in finding it, and, given the context of the passage, that help

---

[2] See commentary on this passage by Frank Fletcher, ed., *Virgil Aeneid VI* (Oxford: Clarendon Press, 1962), pp. 45–46. Also the long, important note of Norden's: E. Norden, *P. Vergilius Maro Aeneis Buch VI* (Leipzig: B. G. Teubner, 1916), pp. 163–179; 189–194. An excellent article on the place of the golden bough in the *Aeneid* is R. Brooks, "*Discolor Aura*. Reflections on the Golden Bough," *A. J. Ph.* LXXIV (1953), 260–280. To all these works I am indebted for my understanding of the simile.

will have to be divine. Associated with the golden bough, then, are the ideas of death, life, concealment, and divine aid. Furthermore, it is by returning the golden bough to Proserpina that Aeneas will make his way safely through the world of the dead to Elysium. That the bough is golden, the metal men dig from the hidden resources of the earth, is connected with Aeneas' descent into the underworld where he, too, will search out hidden resources. The bough then is the magical means whereby Aeneas can both die and not die: he can die spiritually and emotionally to his past at the same time that he can go on living, but in a new manner, in the present and into the future. Moreover, Vergil points out in the simile that the tree on which the mistletoe grows is not its parent; the mistletoe is an additive to the tree, and so is the golden bough on its tree. The point is worth noting, for it implies that when Aeneas plucks the golden bough he is not only revealing himself as a true, legitimate hero, but also adding something to himself, namely divine aid. He is not yet ready to function alone; the hero needs still the help of the gods. Finally, the fact that the bough grows on a tree, like the mistletoe, is also significant, for by this time in the *Aeneid* the tree similes have become symbols for men and cities. Indeed, by plucking the golden bough and bearing it to the world of the dead, Aeneas reveals that he is like the mighty oak tree whose branches reach to heaven and whose roots stretch to Tartarus (IV. 437–449). He takes up the symbol of life, which indicates the hidden spirit of Aeneas, just as the mistletoe on the dormant tree in winter indicates by its presence the hidden life of the tree.

The other simile compares the shades gathered by Cocytus' stream and the Styx to the leaves of a tree and to birds. It is one of the most famous similes in the *Aeneid,* and justifiably so, for through its means the pathos of the situation Vergil describes becomes evident:

> huc omnis turba ad ripas effusa ruebat,
> matres atque viri defunctaque corpora vita
> magnanimum heroum, pueri innuptaeque puellae,
> impositique rogis iuvenes ante ora parentum:
> quam multa in silvis autumni frigore primo
> lapsa cadunt folia, aut ad terram gurgite ab alto
> quam multae glomerantur aves, ubi frigidus annus
> trans pontum fugat et terris immittit apricis.
> stabant orantes primi transmittere cursum,
> tendebantque manus ripae ulterioris amore.
> (VI.305–314)

The enumeration of the dead in an ascending order of pathos helps arouse the sympathy of the audience and prepares the way for the simile. The comparison of the unquiet shades to fallen leaves suggests the countlessness of the dead, their anonymity and equality in death, although they were in life of all classes, types, and ages of humanity. The comparison also indicates the brevity and fragility of life and the inevitability of death. A further, more precise, similarity between the shades and the fallen leaves of a tree lies in the fact that the shades are men already dead, but not yet carried to their final resting place.

But it is not only leaves which these shades are like; they are also like birds who are put to flight by the cold. In both these similes, the cold is comparable to death's chill. But the birds in their flight to warmer lands supply a new note of pathos, for the dead have not been sent to warmer lands; they are still waiting for admittance to Charon's raft. The use of birds as analogues to men, particularly defenseless men, has repeatedly occurred in the first six books of the *Aeneid,* and the accumulation of those passages affects this one. But here alone occurs the equation of birds and leaves comparable to human beings. As a result, the leaf simile acquires force from the bird simile. In both cases, however, the comparison of unburied dead to birds and leaves, things which have inherent in them their own mortality, contributes to the pathos of the passage. Although pathos is the dominant tone in the simile, another more cheerful one is also present, for migrating birds do return in the spring, and, as an analogue for the trans-migrating souls, the implied return of the birds suggests the eventual return of the departed souls to the shores of light.

Two similes of flowers occur in the last six books. Each is used to describe a dead young man, and the two similes are companion pieces. The first compares the death of Euryalus to a purple flower of the poppy:[3]

> volvitur Euryalus leto, pulchrosque per artus
> it cruor inque umeros cervix conlapsa recumbit:
> purpureus veluti cum flos succisus aratro
> languescit moriens, lassove papavera collo
> demisere caput pluvia cum forte gravantur.
>
> (IX.433–437)

Euryalus, the handsome youth, is killed by Volcens, and the blood staining his fair and slowly dying body calls forth the comparison, for

---

[3] See p. 32.

he is like the flower cut by the plow, or even like a flower beaten down by the rain. Not only is Euryalus' appearance as he dies like a flower, but his beauty throughout his life has been like a flower's, and the destruction of such beauty seems wanton. Yet Euryalus himself, as has already been shown, ultimately bears the responsibility for his own death, for it was his desire for glory and fame that led him to the rashness of plundering his slain enemies, and in his death he involves his friend Nisus. Euryalus is not the innocent flower, for all his beauty. Vergil conveys by his simile, viewed in the larger context of the entire Nisus-Euryalus episode, the disparateness between the appearance of Euryalus and his tragic reality. At the same time, he indicates the pathos of misguided loveliness destroyed. From all these involvements, the power of the simile derives, so that we are moved by it and Euryalus' death, at the same time that we perceive and judge the cause of that death.

The companion simile describes the appearance of the slain Pallas, as he appears on his bier, just before he is to be borne back to his father, Euander:

> qualem virgineo demessum pollice florem
> seu mollis violae seu languentis hyacinthi,
> cui neque fulgor adhuc nec dum sua forma recessit,
> non iam mater alit tellus virisque ministrat.
>
> (XI.68–71)

The bier has been filled with boughs, but the dead youth is lovelier by far. The passage obviously echoes that of book VI in which Anchises tells of the funeral of the younger Marcellus (VI. 883–886), and part of the pathos of Pallas' death arises because of that echo. Even in death Pallas' beauty has not yet receded, though the earth does not still nourish him; he has been plucked as a young girl plucks a flower. Pallas died, unlike Euryalus, as a victim of Turnus. He died as a result of a wanton act by a human being, not like Euryalus as the victim of forces which have as their purpose the nurture of the land. But the suggestive quality of the simile is not yet exhausted. By implicitly comparing Turnus to a virginal girl, Vergil shows us that Turnus' stripping of the *cingula* and *balteus* from the slain Pallas was a frivolous, self-gratifying gesture. Turnus wanted those accoutrements as a young girl wants a flower to enhance her beauty. But what is a charming act in a young girl becomes grotesque in a man who acts from a similar motive. The comparison of Turnus to the girl underscores his belief that appearance alone matters, and emphasizes how frivolous Turnus is.

Moreover, the simile also gains power from the fact that Pallas is a type for all the youth who are being cut down by the war raging between Trojan and Latin. As a son of Latin soil fighting on behalf of the Trojans, Pallas summarizes in himself both sides. The echo of the simile used of the dead Euryalus underscores the point. In book VII when the men of Italy are marshalled for Turnus, the repeated language is that of mother earth offering her finest flower (VII. 647 ff.). The horror of the war arises from the very fact that the killing of youth is a desperate thing, from which the land and the people will recover only with difficulty. Pallas, for whom the lamentation and mourning form the central core of the burial of the dead of both sides in book XI, epitomizes this tragic waste.

Yet there is another aspect to Pallas' death, and that is implied in his name. It was in book II that we saw that the theft of the Palladium of Pallas Athena from Troy insured the city's destruction. In book XI, Pallas, who dies for the Trojan cause, is borne back for burial to Euander, whose home is the future site of Rome. As his name suggests, he brings the protection of his spirit, the new Palladium, to the civilization Aeneas is to found, and which will blossom into Roman culture. Even in death he is to be an aid, a beautiful flower, for both Trojan and Latin who will ultimately coalesce into the Roman. The poignancy of the simile derives from the fact of Pallas' death, from the war's destructiveness, and from the future hope Pallas himself is able to give to the Roman civilization. Pallas makes up, as it were, for the irony of Euryalus' death. In death he, like the earlier man, is compared to a flower, but now the flower transcends its earlier ironic limitation.

*Chapter 4*

# Dido and Turnus
# Versus Aeneas

Eight similes in books I, IV, and VI, and two in books VII and VIII refer to Dido, Aeneas, and Turnus. Though the similes have connections with others in the *Aeneid*, they nevertheless deserve separate consideration because they are so closely linked together through Aeneas who appears in both groups as a foil first to Dido and then to Turnus. As Vergil customarily uses similes to define action as well as to illuminate it, so through these similes he reveals the three chief characters of his epic to permit his audience to perceive the springs of their behavior and so be able to judge them.

When Dido first appears in the *Aeneid*, surrounded by a great throng of youth, Vergil uses a simile describing, characterizing, and illuminating her:

> regina ad templum, forma pulcherrima Dido,
> incessit magna iuvenum stipante caterva.
> qualis in Eurotae ripis aut per iuga Cynthi
> exercet Diana choros, quam mille secutae
> hinc atque hinc glomerantur Oreades; illa pharetram
> fert umero gradiensque deas supereminet omnis
> (Latonae tacitum pertemptant gaudia pectus):
> talis erat Dido, talem se laeta ferebat
> per medios instans operi regnisque futuris.
>
> (I.496–504)

Dido is likened to Diana who trains her band, clustered about their queen, on the banks of the Eurotas or along the ridges of Cynthus.[1] As Diana stands out above all the rest, so Dido excels among her Carthaginians. The simile deliberately recalls the appearance of Venus in this same book, who was described in terms of a young Spartan or Thracian maiden who hunts:

> cui mater media sese tulit obvia silva
> virginis os habitumque gerens et virginis arma
> Spartanae, vel qualis equos Threissa fatigat
> Harpalyce volucremque fuga praevertitur Hebrum.
>                                           (I.314–317)

Both scenes stress the beauty of the women, their virginal appearance with its undertone of sexuality, and the notion of the huntress. As a result of his encounter with his mother and her words of encouragement, as well as his own bewildered and anxious state of mind, Aeneas sees the beautiful and compelling Dido as a source of safety, as an almost divine sanctuary for both himself and his men. But neither the goddess of love nor the widowed queen is a virgin. Vergil is at great pains to make the point clear in Aeneas' encounter with Venus, for after telling Aeneas of Dido's first marriage, the goddess reveals in her departure from her son that she is his mother. This revelation of Venus' false appearance suggests that Dido, too, may ultimately reveal herself as different from her initial appearance. And it is this very conflict between Dido's appearance and her reality which the simile of Diana suggests, for Dido is neither a virgin nor a goddess, nor does she hunt as Diana hunts. As she will finally reveal on the hunting expedition (book IV), Dido searches for a man, a husband, a marriage. The simile of Venus as the Spartan huntress prepares the way for the simile of Dido as Diana, and that simile in turn prepares for Dido's tracking of Aeneas, and her attaining of what she calls a *coniugium*. The allusion to Diana, the huntress, finds its realization in the hunting expedition Dido plans for Aeneas' pleasure.

But point of view as an artistic device also enters into Vergil's handling of the Diana simile. For such a comparison to spring to Aeneas' mind reveals how unaware he is; enwrapped as he is in a cloud, he can see only as through a cloud; he sees in effect only what he wants to: a woman who, despite her past suffering, nevertheless appears as a beautiful, nubile, maiden. He fails, as the simile vividly demonstrates, to heed his mother's words that the queen of Carthage is

---

[1] See also pp. 8 ff.

a widow. In organizing Aeneas' view of Dido, Vergil at once reveals his hero's partial awareness and alerts his audience to it.[2] We, unlike Aeneas, are prepared for the ensuing revelations.

Although Vergil borrows this simile from Homer who used it to describe Nausicaa,[3] he so greatly changes its significance as to make it uniquely his own. Our awareness of the Homeric parallel may encourage our awareness of the irony of the simile, but that ironical quality is Vergil's own creation, one we can only understand from Vergil's poem.

The second simile used of Dido occurs in book IV:

> uritur infelix Dido totaque vagatur
> urbe furens, qualis coniecta cerva sagitta,
> quam procul incautam nemora inter Cresia fixit
> pastor agens telis liquitque volatile ferrum
> nescius: illa fuga silvas saltusque peragrat
> Dictaeos; haeret lateri letalis harundo.
>
> (IV.68–73).

The simile continues motifs seen in the first one. Dido, inflamed with passion for Aeneas, wanders madly through the city, just as a doe, struck by the arrow of a shepherd who is unaware of what he has done, wanders wounded through forests and glen. Dido's wound is the wound of her fatal passion for Aeneas, just as the deer's wound will prove fatal (*haeret lateri letalis harundo*). Several things should be observed about this simile and its position in the narrative. First, the phrase *nescius pastor* recalls the *inscius pastor* of the storm simile of book II (304–308).[4] As Aeneas witnessed the havoc wreaked on Troy, he was portrayed as not understanding the reason why; he was only an observer of the event. But in book IV Aeneas, who does not appear in the scene, is utterly unaware of what his very appearance as well as his misfortunes have aroused in Dido's breast. Yet in this simile the *pastor* has nonetheless acted, for it was he who shot the arrow. The change is worth noting, for it suggests that ignorance of one's action does not excuse the responsibility for that action. Furthermore, the use

---

[2] The cloud with which Venus covered Aeneas and Achates as they advanced to Carthage protected them from the gaze of others, but it also symbolized their ignorance of the significance of the past and present. The point is implicitly made when Aeneas views, through his tears as well as through the cloud, the pictures on the walls of the temple. The cloud is furthermore, first called a *nebula* (I. 412) but later a *nubes* (I. 580). The latter word occurs at II. 606 where the context reveals that normal vision is at best a cloud. Venus' cloud of protection seems ill-advised.

[3] Homer, *Odyssey* 6. 102–109.

[4] See pp. 6, 60, 134 ff. on II. 304–308, see pp. 13 ff., 22 ff., 31 ff., 101. See also Newton, 31–43.

of *pastor* stresses, in a sense, the irresponsibility of the action: a *pastor* normally looks after flocks; it is usually not his task to hunt or shoot arrows into deer. The action of the *pastor* in the simile implies the irrelevancy of the act. Aeneas, as book IV will show, acts like this *nescius pastor,* for by acceding to his desire for dalliance he will cost Dido her life, and almost destroy himself and his people.

Next, in the simile the doe, which would prefer not to be wounded, is described as *incautam.* But the epithet is ambiguously applicable to both Dido and the doe. In using the word of the doe, the passive connotation of *incauta* is stressed, but Dido is far more active in her heedlessness. The *incautam* of the simile hints at Dido's responsibility in the unfolding tragedy. A discrepancy exists between the vehicle and the tenor of the simile: the wound may have been inflicted by Aeneas, but it is Dido's own passion, her own desires, which have caused it to fester. The narrative of book IV implied this point before the appearance of the simile. Dido, in her conversation with Anna, paid scrupulous attention to the letter of her vow to remain faithful to Sychaeus, but not to the spirit which prompted that vow. Her will and her desire struggle, as lines 60–66 indicate, and her desire triumphs. The simile, then, explicitly comments on Dido, but appearing as it does near the beginning of the affair, it adumbrates the tangled motives and the shared responsibilities of the tragedy.

But it serves yet another purpose, for like the animal similes already discussed, it emphasizes that Dido's passion reduces her behavior to something like that of an animal. Her passion has made her respond as a wounded animal would, not as a thinking human being. Yet the tone is not the savage one of the wolf simile in book II (355–360); Vergil has softened its impact by appealing to his readers' sympathy for any wounded creature, so that pity is aroused for Dido because of what is both done to her and what she does to herself. The simile's emphasis on the change of Dido from hunter to victim anticipates the hunt itself, which Dido soon organizes for Aeneas' enjoyment and amusement, and in which she will be caught by the snares of her own devising. The doe simile, then, anticipates the one used to describe Aeneas as he sets forth on the expedition:

> ipse ante alios pulcherrimus omnis
> infert se socium Aeneas atque agmina iungit.
> qualis ubi hibernam Lyciam Xanthique fluenta
> deserit ac Delum maternam invisit Apollo
> instauratque choros, mixtique altaria circum
> Cretesque Dryopesque fremunt pictique Agathyrsi;

> ipse iugis Cynthi graditur mollique fluentem
> fronde premit crinem fingens atque implicat auro,
> tela sonant umeris: haud illo segnior ibat
> Aeneas, tantum egregio decus enitet ore.
>
> (IV.141–150)

Briefly and symbolically the simile describes Aeneas' life until he reaches North Africa and Dido's Carthage: the Trojan hero left one place, led a band of people to another, walked along a ridge until he came upon a valley whence he looked down upon others thronging below, and bursts forth like a god. The simile, a companion piece to that used to describe Dido in book I, suggests that Aeneas, likened to Apollo leading the chorus at Delos and to Apollo the hunter, shares some of the characteristics of Dido: both appear amid a throng of others and both stand out for their handsomeness. Furthermore, their lives have run in similar courses: both were forced to flee their home-lands and both are rulers. The appropriateness of similes drawing on the gods who were the twin children of Leto becomes apparent. Indeed, the use of the two similes suggests that there should be a continuing similarity between the lives of Aeneas and Dido. But we know there will not be, for the simile also recalls the one used to describe Aeneas when he first appeared to Dido in book I, where his beauty, enhanced by his mother's skill, was compared to a chryselephantine statue:

> restitit Aeneas claraque in luce refulsit
> os umerosque deo similis; namque ipsa decoram
> caesariem nato genetrix lumenque iuventae
> purpureum et laetos oculis adflarat honores:
> quale manus addunt ebori decus, aut ubi flavo
> argentum Pariusve lapis circumdatur auro.
>
> (I.588–593)

There he was compared to a statue of a god. In book IV he is compared to a god. The change is significant for the role Aeneas is to play opposite Dido. Her passion at this point in the affair has invested him with god-like qualities (cf. IV. 12–13), and so he appears. But it is crucial that the god should be Apollo, for the simile emphasizes the god as the singer and hunter, just as Aeneas has been the singer to Dido of the fall of Troy and his wanderings and is the hunter, not only of beasts as at the moment, but also of a secure haven for himself and his companions. Furthermore, as the phrase *tela sonant umeris* hints, there is an ominous tone to this hunting, ominous specifically for Dido. Apollo is the god of doom (cf. the Homeric "far-darter," *Iliad* I. 43–52), and Aeneas will be the man of doom by being the one who precipitates Dido's own destruction. Vergil, in this simile, catches all these allusions and hints which have so far appeared in the *Aeneid*. But in the very comparison with Apollo, Aeneas becomes almost transcendent. Such a point emphasizes the way he appears to Dido. He will be for her an impossible goal which she can never attain no matter how ardently she might desire it; Aeneas becomes for Dido a god-like creature indeed, whom she might enjoy but never possess, and her failure to observe this last distinction contributes to her own destruction. By itself, the very fact that Dido and Aeneas are compared to Diana and Apollo, children of Leto, suggests the inappropriateness of a union between the Trojan and the Queen of Carthage. Vergil not only involves in his simile what has already happened in the *Aeneid,* but anticipates what will happen, and thereby indicates to his audience how the action is to be observed.

Rumor has made Dido aware that Aeneas is preparing to depart, and Vergil compares her to a bacchante:

> saevit inops animi totamque incensa per urbem
> bacchatur, qualis commotis excita sacris
> Thyias, ubi audito stimulant trieterica Baccho
> orgia nocturnusque vocat clamore Cithaeron.
> (IV.300–303)

This short simile notes that Dido's lack of reason has made her into the mindless, inflamed thing that is the bacchante inspired by the god. However, there still exists that crucial disparity between Dido and the terms of the simile. The bacchante in the simile is inspired *commotis sacris,* and the bacchic rites are religious in origin, whereby the participant becomes joined with the god. But Dido's passion is not religious; it is a passion for a man whom her imagination has transformed into a god. The simile advances our understanding of Dido by forcing on our attention the fact that her reason is in abeyance, that she no longer is able to distinguish between appearance and reality. The ensuing scene between her and Aeneas emphasizes the point. She accuses him of betraying their *coniugium,* and when Aeneas denies that he had ever offered her the hope of marriage, she cannot face the reality of the situation, that the hunted man has eluded her. From now on what had been latent in Dido's character becomes manifest.

Connected with the previous simile is the next in book IV wherein Dido in her mad passion is compared to Pentheus and Orestes:

> agit ipse furentem
> in somnis ferus Aeneas, semperque relinqui
> sola sibi, semper longam incomitata videtur
> ire viam et Tyrios deserta quaerere terra,
> Eumenidum veluti demens videt agmina Pentheus
> et solem geminum et duplices se ostendere Thebas,
> aut Agamemnonius scaenis agitatus Orestes,
> armatam facibus matrem et serpentibus atris
> cum fugit ultricesque sedent in limine Dirae.
>
> (IV.465–473)

In the introduction to the simile, Vergil indicates that to Dido, Aeneas has become *ferus*. She dreams of herself as hunted by a wild beast who drives her mad. The lines pick up the hunting metaphor already employed in earlier similes, and she who once appeared as the hunter now sees herself as the hunted, and the creature she would hunt has become the beast which hunts her. She has transferred to Aeneas the attitude she herself had toward him. In her dreams she further sees herself abandoned, forced to travel alone (no longer the chief member of a throng), and to seek the "Tyrians" in a waste land. The emphasis on Aeneas as beast is like the madness of Pentheus who, in his refusal to acknowledge the power of Bacchus, was driven mad so that he saw two suns and two Thebes. Dido like Pentheus cannot see the actual world; the double visions signify the inability on the part of Pentheus (and Dido) to distinguish appearance from reality. Dido, in her dreams, is also like Orestes, forced to flee the source of danger to herself, but unlike Orestes, Dido's danger comes from herself, not from an armed mother nor from the Dirae.[5] Contained in the simile as well is the clear implication that death is the final way out from the madness, as the phrase *longam . . . ire viam* suggests, and so it anticipates Dido's resolution of her misery. Aeneas, in the light of the simile, has become for Dido a figure of vengeance and of punishment. But when we recall that such an idea operates only within Dido's own mind, and that she is not really the victim of external agents, as were Pentheus and Orestes, we see how she has constructed in fantasy her guilt and suffering, and we see also that she brought about her own plight by her repeated failure to perceive the reality of her situation, i.e., that she is responsible for her own errors. As the reference to Pentheus indicates, her passion has led her to a wholly deluded way of perceiving herself.

---

[5] Vergil indicates in the simile that he is drawing from earlier literature, probably from the plays of Pacuvius, Euripides, and Aeschylus, to align Dido's madness with that of previous victims. See Servii, *Commentarii* (editio Harvardiana), III, *ad* IV. 469, pp. 403–404.

The similes of books I and IV, relating specifically to Dido, illuminate not only her passion and its relationships with previous passions in literature, but also suggest that her own errors lie at the root of her character and participate in her own destruction. If we examine Dido's subsequent behavior, we find confirmation of the evidence of the similes.

Dido first appears in book I as a worthy ruler whom circumstances have forced to assume the role of a man, a king. She has successfully led her people from a dangerous situation to a safe one; she has skillfully avoided the various pitfalls along the way, and when she first appears she is at the peak of her powers. Upon seeing Aeneas for the first time, she is attracted to him and longs to hear of his adventures. But in listening to those tales, which she wants retold often, she fails to understand their full import. Book II makes clear that the fall of Troy came about through a variety of causes, but chief among them was the Trojan's own wilful blindness.[6] Dido, in book IV, never gives evidence of understanding the reasons for Troy's fall nor, subsequently, of her own responsibility for hers. Vergil's use in books I and IV of metaphors derived from the beleaguered city to describe Dido suggests that Dido herself is like Troy, not only in being destroyed, but in contributing to that destruction. By such metaphorical language, Vergil reinforces the similarity between Dido and Troy.[7] Dido's behavior throughout book IV progressively reveals her own self-delusion. Her first conversation with Anna at the opening of the book reveals a queen who behaves as an adolescent. Her unwillingness to admit to herself, or to Anna, what she wants from Aeneas forces Anna to state Dido's most obvious longings. In the confrontation scene with Aeneas, she refuses to admit that he could love her and at the same time leave her. She repeatedly refuses to acknowledge the validity of his claim that he must go to Italy. Even when she sends Anna to plead for a little time, she acts in a self-infatuated manner. Her resolve finally to kill herself is the culmination of her own desire to force the world to her will. The death she plans for herself, and which she finally accomplishes, is in accord with her romantic and sentimental notions of love. In the course of book IV, she has never learned the very thing Aeneas is forced to learn, namely, that love involves responsibility towards others. For example, Aeneas' concern for Iulus and for his men is the turning point in his decision to leave Dido, although he himself is clearly enough satisfied

---

[6] See the discussion of the animal similes on pp. 63 ff.

[7] Newton, 31–43.

to remain. Dido, on the other hand, is incapable of extending that same impulse to Aeneas. Her refusal to recognize his destiny and his responsibility to others and so to himself are symptomatic of her narcissistic love for herself. The love she once felt for Aeneas turns at the end of book IV to bitter hatred and, in invoking the great curse upon Aeneas and his family, Dido becomes the emasculating witch who would destroy what she cannot have. This point is most dramatically presented in her account of the Massylian *sacerdos,* in the description of the funeral pyre she erects, in her placing an effigy of the hero upon it, and in her using his sword to stab herself. Her narcissism which can only admit her view of reality turns not against Aeneas and Iulus, whom she would destroy if she could, but upon herself. Only when she sees Aeneas sail away does the full venom of her self-love spew forth to her own hurt. So long as he remained, no matter how aloof he might be, she could in her own eyes find justification for her actions and attitudes. By arranging Dido's death agony in the fashion he does, Vergil shows us how baneful Dido's delusion is, and how her behavior can lead only to her destruction. For confirmation of this point, we need only turn to the actual death. Dido has plunged the sword into herself but yet does not die. She raises herself three times and falls back three times, and with wandering eyes she searches for the light of the sun and having seen it, she groans (IV. 690–692). Her struggles and her seeking for the light suggest that Dido has discovered too late what she has done.[8] As she seeks the light of heaven and groans, she groans not only at leaving the world of light but also at the enormity of her action. Only then, only after the appearance of light to Dido, does Vergil allow her agony to be ended through the divine intervention of Juno and Iris. Dido had not lived her allotted time nor was her death her proper reward; she dies because of *furor* (IV. 696–699). Dido dies for love, as book VI will make clear (VI. 442 ff.), but a diseased love, one that finally revolves around herself. *Furor,* as Otis remarks, triumphed over *humanitas.*[9]

The discrepancy between appearance and reality of Dido's character is brought out at each crucial stage in the dramatic narrative by a simile which at the same time likens and contradicts the likeness of the queen to something else.

But we have not done with Dido and the similes surrounding her. In book VI two more occur when Aeneas sees Dido in the underworld

---

[8] *Quaesivit* (692) means "she sought for (something)" and bears the connotations of "meditating on something," "trying to gain something."

[9] Otis, p. 269.

and when he leaves her. The two similes frame the appearance of the dead queen:

> inter quas Phoenissa recens a vulnere Dido
> errabat silva in magna; quam Troius heros
> ut primum iuxta stetit agnovitque per umbras
> obscuram, qualem primo qui surgere mense
> aut videt aut vidisse putat per nubila lunam,
> demisit lacrimas dulcique adfatus amore est . . .
>
> (VI.450–455)

The point of view is again that of Aeneas, as in the simile in book I, but unlike those used in book IV. Dido is again amidst a crowd, but she stands out this time only for Aeneas. No longer is she a great, commanding queen, but only one shade among the dead. The verbal echo (454) of the simile used to describe the whole of the underworld serves to emphasize this point (VI. 268–272). To Aeneas, she, who once commanded his life, seems like the moon fitfully seen on cloudy nights. The simile reveals the consequences of Dido's appearance, character, and actions on Aeneas. In so doing, it summarizes the significance of Dido for Aeneas. She was like the moon in being a creature of deceptive appearance, a creature constantly changing. The light Aeneas thought he found turned out to be a false or, at best, a shifting one. The fact that the moon appears in the simile *per nubila* recalls the first time Aeneas saw Dido when he was wrapped in a cloud. The cloud symbolized Aeneas' obscured vision even as now the moon is obscured. The simile makes clear how changeable was Dido's love for Aeneas. The fact, too, that it is the moon to which Dido is compared recalls that Diana was the goddess of the moon and that in another of her aspects Diana is Hecate, who functions in moonlight and to whom Dido offered the sacrifice of her death (IV. 609 ff.). Dido has become identified with an aspect of Diana. Aeneas' own sacrifice to Hecate, before he entered Avernus (VI. 243 ff.), becomes a parallel action to Dido's sacrifice and suggests in view of his encounter with Dido, and in juxtaposition with this simile, that he was unknowingly then sacrificing to Dido in order to appease her as well as Hecate.

The second simile which occurs at the end of the encounter describes Dido as unyielding to Aeneas' final plea to her for understanding. In effect she rejects his "sacrifice":

> illa solo fixos oculos aversa tenebat
> nec magis incepto vultum sermone movetur
> quam si dura silex aut stet Marpesia cautes.
>
> (VI.469–471)

She is compared to a *silex* and to a *cautes,* a flintstone and a sharp rock. The point of the comparison is, of course, to emphasize her hardheartedness, her intransigence, and her unforgiving hatred which would, if it could, still cause him injury or death. The use of *cautes* recalls, too, the *durae . . . cautes* Dido said was Aeneas' birthplace (IV. 366). This recollection underscores the reversal of roles Dido and Aeneas have undergone since their final encounter at Carthage.[10] But, in addition, the simile conveys how terrestrial Dido has been, how like an elemental rock, indifferent, finally, to Aeneas. In this final simile of Dido, Vergil portrays how inhuman Dido's character actually became.[11] The love Dido once thought she felt, or was supposed to feel, for Aeneas turned into a hatred as hard as flint and as murderous as a sharp-edged stone. Her self-love was the rock on which he could well have foundered. Thus, the moon and rock similes reflect the beginning and end of the love affair between Dido and Aeneas.

The importance of Dido to the *Aeneid* lies in her relationship to Aeneas' developing character. She is a test of his character, one he must undergo if he is ever to become the rightful bearer of civilization. In her own turning away from love, she supplies Aeneas with a moral lesson in what love is and is not. Through his experience of Dido, Aeneas discovers what it signifies to love and how love can be the liberating force it should be for the individual. The passage of Aeneas with Dido tests him in offering to him the great temptation to rest content in a childlike security where he will be forever loved but will never be forced to achieve his own destiny. Aeneas' arrival in North Africa (I. 159–169) is descriptive of this security, for Vergil's language is a metaphorical description of the entrance to the womb, that place of elemental security where one need only be and never do. Aeneas' reluctance to leave Dido in book IV, his reluctance to leave his own peace and contentment at Carthage, reinforce the point. But were he to remain with Dido, he would have denied forever his growth and his assumption of the role of manhood. The love Dido offers him is a deluding love, one that arises from her own delusions and that also involves him in delusion, and it eventually becomes, or could become, an emasculating one. Yet it is also a sweet love, one any man, who would be willing to settle only for his own enjoyment, would readily welcome. Were he to do so, he would become a victim and ultimately share in his own

---

[10] Fletcher, p. 66 *ad* 450 ff.

[11] Although it may be argued that Dido's refusal to speak to Aeneas repays his scorning of her, nevertheless it should be noted that Aeneas did reply in his final interview with Dido. However weak his explanation may have appeared, he did try to explain and not insult her with contemptuous silence.

destruction. Dido's love is so destructive because it cannot face reality, specifically the reality or the existence of another human being; for her the other person can only exist on her terms.

If we regard Dido's story only from her point of view, it can easily be looked upon as a tragedy, and recent criticism generally considers Dido a tragic victim.[12] In doing so, critics tend to simplify the complexity of Vergil's creation and to distort its significance by a false emphasis. Dido is culpable, pathetically so. We can feel pity and sympathy for her blindness, as Vergil wants us to; but he also wants us to be aware of her blindness as a moral blindness as well, one which will not heed the clear evidence presented to it or hearken to the reality it confronts. Dido is an active agent in her own destruction. We are expected to judge Dido as well as to feel pity for her. If we do not do so, we fail to understand the crucial importance her role plays in Aeneas' life and in the structure of the *Aeneid*.

Comparable to these similes are two important ones in books VII and VIII respectively, one about Turnus, the other about Aeneas. Their appearance early in the narrative of the last six books and in parallel scenes suggests both that the two men are comparable in behavior and action and that their relationship to one another will be intimately connected. So much we know is true because of our awareness of what finally happens between the two. But it is through the similes that we are given a preview of both the characters and the consequences of the characters of both men.

The first of the two similes occurs in book VII, immediately after Allecto has inspired Turnus to madness:

> arma amens fremit, arma toro tectisque requirit;
> saevit amor ferri et scelerata insania belli,
> ira super: magna veluti cum flamma sonore
> virgea suggeritur costis undantis aëni
> exsultantque aestu latices, furit intus aquai
> fumidus atque alte spumis exuberat amnis,
> nec iam se capit unda, volat vapor ater ad auras.
> (VII.460–466)

The madness and wrath churning within Turnus is like the boiling water in the cauldron which at last issues in black vapor. Turnus him-

---

[12] For example, such it seems to me is Pöschl's point, pp. 66–91; see K. Quinn, *Latin Explorations: Critical Studies in Roman Literature* (New York: Humanities Press, 1963), pp. 29–58; M. C. Covi, "Dido in Vergil's *Aeneid*," *Classical Journal*, LX (1964), 57–60. But cf. Otis, pp. 265–269.

self is the cauldron violently heated by the snake Allecto has pitched upon him. The details of the simile correspond to the inspired condition of the man himself. Gripped by the snake, he is like the cauldron heated by the twigs, powerless to do otherwise. The black cloud which comes forth anticipates the blackness of death which will be the final outcome of Turnus' own rage.

The simile and its context echoes the scene in book II where Aeneas awakens from his sleep, in which the ghost of Hector had appeared to him, to discover Troy in flames. Aeneas then, like Turnus now, madly called for arms, and rage and madness engulfed him (II. 314–317). The fact that we know the consequences of Aeneas' earlier rage affects our understanding of this passage in book VII. Unrestrained *ira* and *furor* can only have disastrous results. So indeed they will have for Turnus. Thus the simile, by harking back to a previous action, also allows a glimpse of what is ultimately to transpire for Turnus and the Latin cause.

The second of the two similes is the first of book VIII and compares the darting thoughts of Aeneas to the light coruscating on water in a bronze basin:

> Talia per Latium. quae Laomedontius heros
> cuncta videns magno curarum fluctuat aestu,
> atque animum nunc huc celerem nunc dividit illuc
> in partisque rapit varias perque omnia versat,
> sicut aquae tremulum labris ubi lumen aënis
> sole repercussum aut radiantis imagine lunae
> omnia pervolitat late loca, iamque sub auras
> erigitur summique ferit laquearia tecti.
>
> (VIII.18–25)

The scene, though like the earlier one laid at night, differs from it in that Aeneas is not beset by anything other than his own thoughts, which, it is true, are worrisome enough. The thoughts are like the reflection of light on the water. In this simile there is no fire causing the water to bubble and boil. What is of concern here is the reflection itself and its glancing from all sides of the room. The fact that light is used as the vehicle for the simile suggests illumination, even though it is fitful illumination appropriate to the darting thoughts of Aeneas. But no black cloud issues forth. The contrast between light and darkness characterizes the two men, for Aeneas unlike Turnus sees his way, fitfully but nevertheless by means of light. Unlike Turnus he is not a welter of wrath and rage for war. Furthermore, in the course of book

VIII, the contrast between dark and light continues, for example, in the tale of Cacus versus Hercules and in the similes which end the book (VIII. 589–591; 622–623). Aeneas has passed beyond the condition Turnus is now in, for his "darkness" of wrath occurred at the fall of Troy.

By these similes, Vergil suggests an inevitable conflict between these two men, and a conflict in which one of the two must perish, since Aeneas and Turnus embody exclusive natures: light versus darkness. At the same time, the similes along with their contexts shed light on the Sibyl's prophecy that a second Achilles will be found in Latium, as well as a second Troy (VI. 88–92). The obvious meaning of her words is that the Latins are like the Greeks and Turnus like Achilles. Indeed the wrath of Turnus supports this notion. But Vergil is not merely imitating Homer, he is deeply engaged in transforming the epic, and one of the ways he does so is by changing his literary inheritance. The Trojans in landing at Latium are like the Greeks coming to Troy. Their intention differs though their action is similar. But the attack of the Latins upon the fortified camp of the Trojans is like the Greek attack upon the city of Troy itself. Both Latins and Trojans share in the comparison to Trojans and Greeks. So also do the heroes. For if Turnus resembles Achilles in respect to the rage and anger, so also does Aeneas, who becomes angered at the death of Pallas just as Achilles did at the death of Patroclus. Furthermore, the parentage of Aeneas, far more than that of Turnus, resembles that of Achilles. Yet differences between Achilles and Aeneas are discernible. Just as Venus is a greater deity than Thetis, so Aeneas is not a culpable agent in the death of Pallas as Achilles was in the death of Patroclus.[13] Moreover, it is not Aeneas' purpose to destroy civilization or even to test the heroic code; he has come to transform society and to create civilization. Thus, though both Turnus and Aeneas share in resemblances to Achilles, they also differ. So too in the similes. The two similes used of Turnus and Aeneas are comparable and suggestive of parallels to the hero of the *Iliad,* but both differ from that figure: Turnus for the worse, Aeneas for the better. The Sibyl's prophecy then is true, but true with a difference. Aeneas will discover that both Turnus and himself are like Achilles.

Turnus, like Dido, is frequently considered a tragic figure, one who suffers cruelly at the hands of Aeneas. But such a view of him

---

[13] Achilles did not prevent Patroclus from wearing his armor or even from going off to battle.

seems mistaken, for as we shall see in the discussion of the similes of book XII, Vergil did not so regard him or intend his readers to do so. But even before that discussion it can be shown, albeit tentatively, that Turnus' blindness, folly, and self-delusion lie at the root of his *furor*. The animal similes have already clearly enough indicated that Turnus' perceptions and responses to events are those, often, of a maddened beast, maddened either by a wound or by his own desires. Furthermore, in the similes just discussed and in their juxtaposition, it can be seen how fundamentally different Turnus is from Aeneas. But these distinctions will come clearer in the last chapter.

Turnus is like Dido, and against both of them is set Aeneas. His character and worth are known to us from the fact that he serves as foil to them. We see him in effect because of them. Against their ambiguousness, he stands out even as he did in the first simile used of him in the *Aeneid* (I. 589–593) where he is compared to a chryselephantine statue. Often it has been remarked that Aeneas is a shadowy figure, lacking in personality, presented in only a sketchy fashion. A reading of the text does not support such arguments, as Otis has shown in his recent work. Aeneas is a complex, artfully conceived character whose presence dominates the entire poem. Even as foil to Dido and Turnus, he functions as the figure against whom they are finally judged and found wanting. It is true that Vergil took enormous risks in the presentation of his hero, but at no point is the presence of that hero unfelt; even in the similes we are constantly aware of him.

*Chapter 5*

# Gods and Men

In book I, two similes appear in which gods are compared to human beings: Neptune as statesman; Venus as Spartan maiden. Both similes have already been discussed.[1] Similarly, in books I and IV, Dido and Aeneas are compared to the deities, Apollo and Diana, and the significance of the similes has been canvassed. But Vergil did not rest content with these. In the last half of the *Aeneid,* he again employs the pattern of comparing a god to mankind, and mankind to deities or creatures from mythology. The repetition of the pattern is instructive.

In book VIII, Vulcan arises from Venus' bed to order his Cyclopes to create the divine armor for Aeneas. The way in which he goes about his task is compared to the way a housewife orders her domestic staff:

> Inde ubi prima quies medio iam noctis abactae
> curriculo expulerat somnum, cum femina primum,
> cui tolerare colo vitam tenuique Minerva
> impositum, cinerem et sopitos suscitat ignis
> noctem addens operi, famulasque ad lumina longo
> exercet penso, castum ut servare cubile
> coniugis et possit parvos educere natos:
> haud secus ignipotens nec tempore segnior illo
> mollibus et stratis opera ad fabrilia surgit.
>
> (VIII.407–415)

The simile not only vividly anticipates what Vulcan is about to do but also maintains the tone of sophisticated amusement which surrounds

---

[1] See pp. 20 ff., 90 ff.

the entire conjunction of Venus and Vulcan. Vulcan as housewife fittingly continues the reversal of roles with which the scene began: he is deliberately compared to a woman who goes about her matronly duties, just as Venus played the man's role in seducing Vulcan to her will. The episode lightens the book by casting these Olympian deities in seemingly incongruous roles. The immortals are here indulging in mortal ways. For the first time in the *Aeneid,* gods are treated with humor.

But Vergil also achieves something else by this simile and episode. Venus' purpose is a worthwhile, and, indeed, an imperative one: armor to protect her son. Her object is of utmost seriousness and the simile emphasizes this seriousness, for, after all, running a household is a serious business, even if it lacks the excitement or glamor of making love. Vulcan goes about his tasks with full awareness of this, as his orders to the Cyclopes emphasize:

> 'tollite cuncta' inquit 'coeptosque auferte labores,
> Aetnaei Cyclopes, et huc advertite mentem:
> arma acri facienda viro. nunc viribus usus,
> nunc manibus rapidis, omni nunc arte magistra.
> praecipitate moras.'
>
> (VIII.439–443)

By coupling amusing means to serious ends, Vergil emphasizes the paradox that from opposites, opposites come; from frivolous things come great things, from banal, daily tasks come great tasks, from bad, good, from good, bad. The motif is recurrent throughout the *Aeneid,* e.g., from Ascanius' hunting of the deer arises the war between Latins and Trojans; from the fall of Troy comes the rise of Rome; from the dalliance of Aeneas and Dido arises the death of Dido and the emotional growth of Aeneas. But, significantly, only the gods are presented in so light a mode as they appear here, and, indeed, only these gods. Mortals never attain this sort of sophisticated treatment in the *Aeneid.* The reason, no doubt, is to be found in the fact that the immortal gods were just that, immortal. Death could not touch them, whereas death is ever present for human beings (cf. X. 466 ff.). Their behavior must be regarded seriously at all times, for they continually tread on the brink of death.

The distinction between gods and men lies at the heart of the simile describing Vulcan's passion for Venus:

> dixerat et niveis hinc atque hinc diva lacertis
> cunctantem amplexu molli fovet. ille repente

accepit solitam flammam, notusque medullas
intravit calor et labefacta per ossa cucurrit,
non secus atque olim tonitru cum rupta corusco
ignea rima micans percurrit lumine nimbos.
(VIII.387–392)

Passion as flame has appeared in the Dido-Aeneas encounter, but with disastrous consequences. Here the flame, so often destructive throughout the *Aeneid*, serves finally to inflame Vulcan to fulfill Venus' wish. It does not destroy the god, for passion is incapable of destroying an immortal. The entire episode of Venus and Vulcan recapitulates the tale of Dido and Aeneas, but with the roles of male and female reversed and with the ends reversed. Vulcan leaves his bed of love to pursue his tasks like a good spouse, whereas Dido mounted her bed of love and died. But in addition, Vulcan enflamed symbolizes the flame that will forge the shield, the emblem of the future of Rome. The creative fire, which in effect makes Rome, complements the destructive fire which destroyed Troy and Dido.

An instructive simile of a god disguised as a mortal occurs when Apollo appears as Butes to Ascanius:

. . . forma tum vertitur oris
antiquum in Buten. hic Dardanio Anchisae
armiger ante fuit fidusque ad limina custos;
tum comitem Ascanio pater addidit. ibat Apollo
omnia longaevo similis vocemque coloremque
et crinis albos et saeva sonoribus arma,
atque his ardentem dictis adfatur Iulum:
(IX.646–652)

The protective and paternal quality of Apollo's disguise is immediately obvious, for Ascanius is not to tempt too far his youthful strength; he is not to become a rash warrior such as Nisus or Euryalus. Apollo is pleased by the youth's courage, but properly admonishes Ascanius to cease. Ascanius' obligation is to the future, and, in order to be prepared for it, he must still learn *virtus* and *labor* and not to trust to *fortuna* (cf. XII. 435–436).

Aeneas himself had once been similarly admonished by Mercury:

Aeneas celsa in puppi iam certus eundi
carpebat somnos rebus iam rite paratis.
huic se forma dei vultu redeuntis eodem
obtulit in somnis rursusque ita visa monere est,

> omnia Mercurio similis, vocemque coloremque
> et crinis flavos et membra decora iuventa:
>
> (IV.554–559)

Aeneas needed at that point in his career the guidance of the gods, for his delaying at Carthage still held the possibility of danger for him and his men. That Mercury, messenger of Jupiter, should give such a warning is appropriate (243 ff.); that Vergil should repeat the motif in conjunction with Ascanius suggests that Vergil is implying in the Mercury passage that Aeneas, at that point, needed still to learn of *virtus* and *labor* and to distrust *fortuna*.

But mortals acting as immortals need always to be on their guard. The motif begins in a passage in the catalogue of Latin heroes, where the brothers Catillus and Coras, Argive youths, are compared to the Centaurs:

> Tum gemini fratres Tiburtia moenia linquunt,
> fratris Tiburti dictam cognomine gentem,
> Catillusque acerque Coras, Argiva iuventus,
> et primam ante aciem densa inter tela feruntur:
> ceu duo nubigenae cum vertice montis ab alto
> descendunt Centauri Homolen Othrymque nivalem
> linquentes cursu rapido; dat euntibus ingens
> silva locum et magno cedunt virgulta fragore.
>
> (VII.670–677)

The simile compares their arrival to that of the Centaurs, emphasizing how nature yields before them. The only other time, however, that the word *nubigenae* appears in the *Aeneid* is with reference to Hercules as slayer of the Centaurs:

> . . . 'tu nubigenas, invicte, bimembris,
> Hylaeumque Pholumque manu, tu Cresia mactas
> prodigia et vastum Nemeae sub rupe leonem.
>
> (VIII.293–295)

One would think that Vergil somewhere would indicate the death of Catillus and Coras, but he does not; indeed they fight well (cf. XI. 604 ff.; 640 ff.). What Vergil may be suggesting, by the reference to the Centaurs, is that these men, Catillus and Coras, may in time be changed from their semibestial nature.

But in general mortals acting as divine creatures need to take care, even Aeneas. In book X, Aeneas after learning of Pallas' death rages in his search for Turnus:

> Aegaeon qualis, centum cui bracchia dicunt
> centenasque manus, quinquaginta oribus ignem
> pectoribusque arsisse, Iovis cum fulmina contra
> tot paribus streperet clipeis, tot stringeret ensis:
> sic toto Aeneas desaevit in aequore victor
> ut semel intepuit mucro.
>
> (X.565–570)

Aeneas' anger makes him into a monster like the hundred-armed creatures who opposed Jupiter. The comparison aptly describes the havoc
which the frenzied hero causes. But the simile also hints at dire consequences for such frenzy. Aegaeon finally succumbed to Jupiter's superior power and lies chained beneath Mount Aetna. At the point the
simile occurs, Aeneas has descended to barbarism, understandably, perhaps, but nonetheless dangerously. He treads upon an abyss of destruction and unless he recovers himself, he and those dependent on him
may well suffer. By having Aeneas vent his fury on Mezentius, Vergil
skillfully delays Aeneas' slaying of Turnus until his hero can act in full
awareness of what he is doing. Aeneas, in book X, acts like a monster
and specifically like an immortal one, and such presumption from even
the great hero could not be long borne.

The repetition of this theme of presumption reappears in book X
at the point where Mezentius is about to encounter Aeneas:

> At vero ingentem quatiens Mezentius hastam
> turbidus ingreditur campo. quam magnus Orion,
> cum pedes incedit medii per maxima Nerei
> stagna viam scindens, umero supereminet undas,
> aut summis referens annosam montibus ornum
> ingrediturque solo et caput inter nubila condit,
> talis se vastis infert Mezentius armis.
>
> (X.762–768)

The simile emphasizes Mezentius as a giant, but Mezentius turns out to
be of human dimensions. The comparison of the scorner of the gods
to Orion, the translated hunter, who was also a *monstrum,* as the repetition of line 767 from the Fama passage of book IV (177) indicates, in
itself implies the doom Mezentius is shortly to undergo, for mighty as
he is, he finally will fall before one who is mightier; he will not become
a heavenly constellation, for he is a *monstrum* of human proportions.
The details of the simile recall the appearance of Neptune in book I
who also overcame waves of water. This reminiscence again underscores
the difference between Mezentius and the creatures of the immortal
world. By comparing Mezentius in this way, Vergil both reinforces

the hybris of Mezentius and anticipates his death. Mortals are not immortal, but for them to behave so is to court disaster, as all ancient literature insists upon.

An analogous simile occurs in conjunction with Camilla. Though not concerned with divine creatures, it nonetheless draws upon mythology, heroic mythology. Camilla and her band of warriors are compared to Amazons in book XI:

> at circum lectae comites, Larinaque virgo
> Tullaque et aeratam quatiens Tarpeia securim,
> Italides, quas ipsa decus sibi dia Camilla
> delegit pacisque bonas bellique ministras:
> quales Threiciae cum flumina Thermodontis
> pulsant et pictis bellantur Amazones armis,
> seu circum Hippolyten seu cum se Martia curru
> Penthesilea refert, magnoque ululante tumultu
> feminea exsultant lunatis agmina peltis.
> (XI.655–663)

Camilla's first appearance in the *Aeneid* occurs in book VII, where the description of both her and of the Latins' reaction to her clearly alludes to the Amazons (VII. 803 ff.), and recalls the picture of Penthesilea which Aeneas saw in Juno's temple at Carthage (I. 490–493). But the simile also recalls a motif found in the first description of Camilla in book VII. There she is described as moving swifter than the winds, as though she flew above the grass or grain so that she did not touch them with her feet (VII. 807–811). The passage derives from Homer's description of Ate (*Iliad* XIX. 92–93) and Agathon's description of Eros in Plato's *Symposium* (195D 1–9). Plato deliberately has Agathon use the Homeric description of Ate for his conception of love to call ironic attention to Agathon's sentimental view of Eros, for if love were as Agathon alleges, it would indeed be a creature of mischief. Homer's description of Ate characterizes the folly and delusion which are the essential qualities of Ate. The echoes of Homer and Plato are present in Vergil's description of Camilla, the warrior maiden who forsakes love and all its works to become a creature of mischief in fighting against the Aeneadae and a victim of her own delusion. But it is only in her death that the full implications of the irony become apparent. Camilla's death arises from her essential femininity which she has been at such pains to deny. Her impulse towards love, denied by herself, turns inward so that like Dido she loves only herself. The simile in book XI makes evident how like a man Camilla, the maiden, is. Such an

inversion of roles can only lead to her destruction, for Camilla pre-
sumes to act as though she were by nature something she is not. The
simile reflects her Amazonian quality at the same time it recalls the
self-involvement of Hippolytus. Penthesilea and Hippolytus are para-
digms of Camilla's own character.

These similes show the hybristic nature of the men involved in the
war between Trojans and Latins. All attempt to emulate or even to be
something they are not, and as human beings they, with the exception
of Aeneas, die as a result; they lack the immortality vouchsafed the
gods. These similes, furthermore, make it clear that the gods are capable
of behaving like human beings without any dire consequences to themselves. The comparison of the two beings implies that morality is rooted
not necessarily in devotion to the gods, but in the awareness of mortality. As a consequence, for men to live in accord with their own limitations and in accord with their own potentialities is their highest good.
It is in man's own life that he finds the figure in the carpet, the pattern
of his own existence. It is from his own behavior, and his awareness of
that behavior, that moral results spring. The gods do not determine
man's world in the *Aeneid,* man himself does. This essential point the
similes by their implicit as well as explicit references make clear.

The comparisons of human beings to divinities which occurred in
books I–IV are balanced by similar comparisons in books X–XI, so also
are the similes which compare gods to human beings. The pattern
begun in books I and IV continues in the second half of the *Aeneid.*
But in general the effect is considerably lessened, for Vergil in the second half of his poem does not, with one exception, define his major
characters with such similes.

*Chapter 6*

# The City

The theme of the city, its founding and its building, occupies a considerable space in the *Aeneid*. Book I portrays the growth of Carthage just as book II witnesses the destruction of Troy. For Aeneas the establishment of civilization in the west is intimately connected with his establishing a city and home for the Trojan remnant. When he visits Euander he sees at last the site of the future Rome, and it is at this point that the divine armor is given to him so that he may achieve his goal. The connection between the city and civilization, between the city and its men, preoccupies Aeneas from book I through book XII. Having seen the destruction of his original home, he passionately longs for a new home.

Not surprisingly, there are similes which derive from the theme of the city. But perhaps what is surprising is how few they are in number and how they are used. In almost every instance where the motif of the city appears in a simile, the simile itself is used to describe a human being. The similes make abundantly clear how intertwined men and cities are: the defense of one is, in a sense, the defense of the other; and the attack of one is the attack of the other. Such a pattern the first simile involving a city demonstrates. It is the final simile of book IV, and describes the effect of Dido's death:

> it clamor ad alta
> atria: concussam bacchatur Fama per urbem.
> lamentis gemituque et femineo ululatu
> tecta fremunt, resonat magnis plangoribus aether,
> non aliter quam si immissis ruat hostibus omnis

> Karthago aut antiqua Tyros, flammaeque furentes
> culmina perque hominum volvantur perque deorum.
> (IV.665–671)

From the accumulations of references to cities in previous passages of the poem, this one derives its force.[1] The city at the fall of its queen is like the city laid open to a horde of invaders, and the simile vividly recalls the destruction of Troy where groans, feminine lamentations, fire, and havoc mingled in confusion. But unlike Troy, Carthage is not being invaded, and its ruler has not been struck down by an enemy. Although Vergil points up the similarity between the two cities and the two rulers, he does so to remind us of the difference between them. Dido's death comes about by her own hand and as a consequence of her own faults. She, unlike Priam, has been at the mercy not of hostile Greeks, but of her own emotions. Her city's failure has been a direct consequence of her own failure. The city which Aeneas saw growing before his eyes in book I has now ceased to advance, and the simile clearly identifies Dido with the city. It is because of her and her suicide that Carthage is brought to such a state; its growth has been stopped short by its ruler.

The next simile of the city occurs in book V during the boxing match between Dares and Entellus:

> stat gravis Entellus nisuque immotus eodem
> corpore tela modo atque oculis vigilantibus exit.
> ille, velut celsam oppugnat qui molibus urbem
> aut montana sedet circum castella sub armis,
> nunc hos, nunc illos aditus, omnemque pererrat
> arte locum et variis adsultibus inritus urget.
> (V.437–442)

Dares attacks Entellus much as an invader tries to attack an impregnable city or a well-fortified guardhouse. In comparing Entellus' resistance to a protected city, Vergil makes explicit what he had implied in the previous simile of the city in conjunction with Dido's suicide. The simile is appropriate, not only because it vividly portrays the action occurring in the boxing match and because ultimately Entellus will triumph over Dares, but also because the heart of the city is to be found in its men, men such as Entellus. Entellus represents the type of man who both preserves and fosters the city with his forbearance, strength, and wisdom. He is unlike Dido who lacked those very qualities neces-

---

[1] Especially from the references to Troy as well as Carthage in books I–IV.

sary for the safeguarding of her own city, and whose suicide caused havoc to her own people. If we accept the equation of man as city, we can see how Vergil here in the simile for Entellus comments both on the present action and on Dido's earlier failure. Entellus as the prototype of the man who is the basis of civilization—of life lived in a city— anticipates what Aeneas himself will be.

A curious simile, related to the notion of the city, occurs in book VIII at the site of Rome. It is appropriate in its context, for Euander describes Cacus' cave laid open by Hercules as Hades gaping:

> at specus et Caci detecta apparuit ingens
> regia, et umbrosae penitus patuere cavernae,
> non secus ac si qua penitus vi terra dehiscens
> infernas reseret sedes et regna recludat
> pallida, dis invisa, superque immane barathrum
> cernatur, trepident immisso lumine Manes.
> (VIII.241–246)

The confusion and deadliness of the monster's cave is neatly compared to the dark doom of Hades itself. But because Cacus' cave is near the site of the future Rome, the simile acquires an added connotation. Cacus and his cave represent the very antithesis of what Rome is to be and what Aeneas' own mission is. The establishment of civilization and of the city of Rome will overcome the dark confusion of Cacus' cave and will be an attempt to overcome the limitations of Hades itself, for in the continuity of civilization will be found the only kind of immortality open to mankind. Hercules' destruction of Cacus prefigures Aeneas' own arrival in Latium, for both bring order to chaos. But Aeneas brings not only order to the people of Latium and ultimately to Rome, he provides as well the means of surmounting the dark underworld of the dead. In its context, the simile calls to mind not only the past, which had through the monster afflicted the surrounding peoples, but the future as well. The chaos of Hades laid open in the simile on Cacus' cave is the appropriate antithesis of the life of civilization of the city.

In book IX, Bitias falls at Turnus' hand and his fall is compared to the crumbling of masonry at Baiae:

> talis in Euboico Baiarum litore quondam
> saxea pila cadit, magnis quam molibus ante
> constructam ponto iaciunt, sic illa ruinam
> prona trahit penitusque vadis inlisa recumbit;
> (IX.710–713)

The simile re-emphasizes the connection between the city and the men who inhabit it. Bitias falls just as outworn buildings do, and the simile implies that Bitias, like old masonry, needs to fall if there is to be a new city built, for he, in helping Pandarus open the gates of the Trojan camp, demonstrated his unwillingness to accept the order Aeneas is in the process of establishing. The simile concentrates on the fall, not on Turnus who causes the fall, and indicates that internal forces operate as well as external ones. Bitias, like Turnus and other warriors in book IX, is willing to sacrifice the future, the prospect of civilization, for the sake of his own glory and fame. In this he is not unlike Dido whose motives were all to be found in her own desires. The coupling of their destructive impulses with similes of the city reinforces not only the similarity between the two characters, but also the similarity of their ultimate denial of the city.

One final simile remains to be connected with this group of similes. Although not a simile whose vehicle derives from the city, it is nonetheless appropriate here. In book X, Ascanius is compared to a rare jewel:

> ipse inter medios, Veneris iustissima cura,
> Dardanius caput, ecce, puer detectus honestum,
> qualis gemma micat fulvum quae dividit aurum,
> aut collo decus aut capiti, vel quale per artem
> inclusum buxo aut Oricia terebintho
> lucet ebur; fusos cervix cui lactea crinis
> accipit et molli subnectens circulus auro.
>
> (X.132–138)

The simile occurs amidst the description of Ascanius surrounded by the Trojans in their besieged camp. As the simile makes clear, he is the protected jewel whose safety is a concern both to the men and to Venus. The camp with its defenses is like a city, and at its center is the son of the hero whose mission is to establish a city. Ascanius is the precious jewel, for he represents the future, and particularly the future of the city, for it will be his task to found Alba Longa, the city whence Rome itself will spring. The core of the city is its continuity, represented here by the young Ascanius. The reason for the city, for its protection and increase by its inhabitants, then, is the possibility of the future, the continuance of civilization, and it is this which is the great jewel. For this the city is founded and preserved, even at the cost of death to individual men. Later in book XII a parallel simile involving a jewel will occur, and it too will be related to these similes of the city.

The similes of the city indicate that the city itself is made up of men who are its reason for being and its hope for the future. The city becomes the source of civilization because it allows for the peaceful and harmonious development of organized social life. At the same time, the city and its culture afford the one means for ancient men to escape the limitations of death itself, for it is only through the city that the possibility of immortality of a race or a nation exists. Furthermore, the city gives men their identity. Aeneas' longing for his city in book I, as he watches Carthage growing, underscores his own isolation and the painful deprivation the loss of his home has caused. To realize himself, the individual man needs the city which gives him the means, i.e., the presences of other men and a communal task, for the discovery of himself. But in addition to these aspects, the similes convey the consequences of the destruction of men and their connection with the city. To destroy life, as Dido and Turnus do, is to destroy the city itself, civilization, and the possibility of the future. It is in effect to destroy the jewel of great price. To do as Turnus and Dido do is to permit the chaos of death to triumph, for civilization itself is destroyed. The similes which derive from the powerful motif of establishing civilization in the west illuminate and explore the significance of that motif.

## *Chapter 7*

## The End of the War:
## Book XII

As the narrative of the *Aeneid* reaches its climax in book XII, all of the basic themes of the similes draw together to comment on the attitudes and actions of the chief characters, Aeneas and Turnus, as well as on the victims of the war, the Trojans and Latins.

Book XII opens with Turnus who, upon seeing the Latins disheartened, agrees to single combat with Aeneas. By at last accepting such a trial, he raises the spirits of his followers. Immediately a simile follows, the first of the book, which compares Turnus' violence to a lion who recovers his strength in spite of his wound:

> Turnus ut infractos adverso Marte Latinos
> defecisse videt, sua nunc promissa reposci,
> se signari oculis, ultro implacabilis ardet
> attollitque animos. Poenorum qualis in arvis
> saucius ille gravi venantum vulnere pectus
> tum demum movet arma leo, gaudetque comantis
> excutiens cervice toros fixumque latronis
> impavidus frangit telum et fremit ore cruento:
> haud secus accenso gliscit violentia Turno.
>
> (XII.1–9)

At first glance the simile suggests that the recovered spirits of the Latins are like the renewed lion, for it is not until line 9 that Vergil makes clear what the tenor of the simile is. At that point, we realize that the *violentia* of Turnus, which had been impaired ever since his dereliction in leaving the battlefield in book X, has recovered itself, even as the spirits of the men are recovered; the call for combat with Aeneas rouses both *violentia* and courage. The simile, moreover, by its details— the reference to Phoenician fields, the wounded breast—are reminiscent of Carthage and Dido. The wound Dido endured and Turnus endures is of the heart, and involves their self-esteem; furthermore, each wound came about through Juno's contrivance and has serious consequences for her followers. In addition, the wound is connected with Aeneas: in each instance Aeneas has been the hunter, for Aeneas seemed to Dido to hunt her, and in actuality does hunt Turnus. Although both are characterized by similes of wounded animals, a distinction between the similes is observable since Turnus as the lion is *impavidus*, unlike Dido as the doe which was *incautam;* the implication is that Turnus may fare better than did Dido.

In the light of the similes of wounded animals, and especially in the light of the similes of lions, the simile conveys the notion that hope of eventual recovery and victory for Turnus is at best minimal. Turnus' *violentia* which savages all before it is comparable to the lion-like savagery of Euryalus (IX. 339–342). Turnus himself in book IX (791–796) had been spoken of as a wounded lion who turns upon his attackers, and again in book X (453–456) he was like a lion in attacking Pallas. Also in book X (723–729) Mezentius shortly before his death had been compared to a lion. All the implications of rage, mighty and destructive, contained in the previous similes are alluded to here. As in those similes, where the notion of mindless savage force predominated, so here Turnus' *violentia* compared to the *impavidus leo* embraces the same idea. The ensuing scene in which both Latinus and Amata implore Turnus to lay aside his recklessness dramatically explores the implications of the simile. Appearing early in book XII, the simile characterizes Turnus, adumbrates much of the action of the book, and suggests by its allusion to previous similes the final issue: the lion relying on its savagery, eventually will fall to the weapons of the hunters.

Because of the fact that the lion is a wounded noble beast and therefore arouses the reader's admiration for its courage, the simile evokes sympathy for Turnus and his *violentia*. Vergil reinforces that sympathy by describing the damaging weapon as that of a *latro,* a word which occurs only here in the *Aeneid*. The suggestion is that it is a weapon of a "servant," a "brigand," a "common soldier." The point of view of the simile favors Turnus and deliberately fosters the illusion that Turnus is a noble, though wounded, creature attacked by what appears to be an inferior man. But Aeneas is not a *latro,* in the sense of "brigand," nor is he a *praedo*.[1] The elevation of Turnus and the seeming down-grading of Aeneas is part of Vergil's strategy in this book. For by the end of the book, sympathetic though we may be with Turnus, we are forced to realize that Aeneas is morally and intellectually his superior, and that his final act is right.

In the following episode, Amata pleads with Turnus and announces that she will never look upon Aeneas as her son-in-law. Lavinia hears these words and blushes. Vergil employs a significant simile to describe the maiden whose appearance inflames Turnus with love for the girl:

> accepit vocem lacrimis Lavinia matris
> flagrantis perfusa genas, cui plurimus ignem
> subiecit rubor et calefacta per ora cucurrit.
> Indum sanguineo veluti violaverit ostro
> si quis ebur, aut mixta rubent ubi lilia multa
> alba rosa, talis virgo dabat ore colores.
> illum turbat amor figitque in virgine vultus.
>
> (XII.64–70)

Within its context it describes accurately the look of the young girl and hints as well at the violence done her by her mother's words.[2] But the simile is obviously parallel to the jewel simile used of Ascanius in book X (132–138) which also mentioned ivory, since the appearance of Lavinia is like a valuable colored ivory and like the appearance of roses mixed with lilies. Furthermore, her beauty compared to a work of art or to delicate flowers suggests her value and importance; she is the still center around which the fighting rages, the ultimate goal of both Aeneas and Turnus. The protection surrounding her is like the defense of Ascanius in book X. By implying the comparable value of Lavinia and Ascanius, the two similes highlight the fact that the war between Trojans and Latins is fought for each of them, since through them the future will come to pass.

Concluding the episode of Turnus and Latinus' court is a simile which describes Turnus about to start off for single combat with Aeneas:

> his agitur furiis, totoque ardentis ab ore
> scintillae absistunt, oculis micat acribus ignis,

---

[1] Cf. Putnam, p. 154. He properly draws attention to the uniqueness of *latro*, but in connecting it with *praedo* he fails to note that only enemies of Aeneas use the term. I am indebted to Putnam's chapter, but I disagree with his conclusions and often with his interpretations.

[2] Amata shows herself here as she has in book VII more than a little in love with Turnus; her behavior towards the innocent Lavinia is dubious in the extreme.

mugitus veluti cum prima in proelia taurus
terrificos ciet aut irasci in cornua temptat
arboris obnixus trunco, ventosque lacessit
ictibus aut sparsa ad pugnam proludit harena.

(XII.101–106)

The simile compares Turnus to a roaring bull which tries its horns on
a tree trunk and fights against the wind in preparation for a contest
with another creature. Turnus, like the bull, rages forth confident in
what he is about to do. Such is the immediate effect of the simile. But
closely considered, the simile reveals that the bull achieves nothing,
for his movements are essentially meaningless. In its details, the simile
anticipates the futility of what Turnus is going to do, and so the folly
of that behavior. The bull, like Turnus, gains no victory. The effect of
the simile is somewhat comic, for Turnus as bull achieves sound and
fury signifying in the end nothing.

The simile draws on the previous two bull similes of the poem, the
first used of Laocoon and the second of Pallas. In both previous
instances, the bull was destroyed much as the ox was destroyed by
Entellus in book V. The recurrence here of a simile of a bull reinforces
the notion implicit in the simile itself that Turnus is going forth not
to triumph but to destruction. He will become, by the end of the book,
the creature sacrificed to the past for the sake of the future.

The similes which open and close the episode described in lines
1–106 portray Turnus as an animal; they suggest that as he is about to
engage Aeneas in single combat he is like a creature who only responds
to a stimulus, a creature which cannot take thought for the future or
indeed for any goal other than the satisfaction of an immediate desire.
Turnus' *violentia* and his fury prevent him from looking beyond the
present and so compel him to respond as an animal. The similes suggest
there is little hope for the champion of the Latins. By their position
in the episode the similes form a ring about it, but it is a ring of animals which have only strength and force; they seem capable of defending themselves and others, even as Turnus seems capable of defending
the valuable prize, Lavinia. Ultimately, they suggest that Turnus will
fail against a superior creature such as man. The similes by framing
the episode define its chief protagonist.

But the single combat is long delayed, for Tolumnius, inspired
by Juturna, the agent of Juno, breaks the truce and chaos results.
Aeneas, dismayed, tries valiantly to withstand the frenzy of both the
Latins and his own men. However, he is wounded and forced to with-
draw for a time from battle. Turnus, observing his enemy's departure,

leaps into his chariot and begins to bestrew the field with corpses. Near
the beginning of his action he is compared to Mavors:

> qualis apud gelidi cum flumina concitus Hebri
> sanguineus Mavors clipeo increpat atque furentis
> bella movens immittit equos, illi aequore aperto
> ante Notos Zephyrumque volant, gemit ultima pulsu
> Thraca pedum circumque atrae Formidinis ora
> Iraeque Insidiaeque, dei comitatus, aguntur:
> talis equos alacer media inter proelia Turnus
> fumantis sudore quatit, miserabile caesis
> hostibus insultans; spargit rapida ungula rores
> sanguineos mixtaque cruor calcatur harena.
>
> (XII.331–340)

Turnus' appearance in battle is, indeed, not unlike the god of war driv-
ing his chariot and horses before Notus and Zephyrus. The land groans
even as does Thrace beaten by the horses of the god whose companions
are Fear, Anger, Treachery. The simile is vivid of Turnus' destruction
of the Trojans. But the effect of the simile does not rest solely in its
appositeness to what Turnus is presently doing, for it recalls two other
motifs found in earlier similes. The first, and most obvious, is the comparing of Turnus to Mavors, Mars, the God of War. As has already
been shown, whenever a hybristic human being is compared to an
immortal his death soon follows. Such happened with Mezentius compared to Orion, Mezentius who once had taken the place of Turnus in
battle and had died at Aeneas' hand. Now Turnus at the start of his
final day rages the way Mezentius did and is compared to an immortal
as once Mezentius had been. The implication is clearly that Turnus
will suffer the fate of Mezentius.

But before he does so he strews carnage about him. That behavior
brings up the second point of the simile. In the simile the horses of
Mars are described as flying about the open sea—*aequore ponto;* the
horse of Turnus has also been described as scattering bloody dew on the
land while the land itself becomes sand, mixed with gore. Such descriptions suggest that the plain on which the battle is being fought is
analogous to the sea and the storm raised on it:[3] the motif had been
anticipated earlier, for at the outbreak of the conflict the weapons were
described as a storm and a rainfall of iron (XII. 283–285). The transforming of the plain into a sea of battle recurs deliberately in following similes and episodes and is clearly designed to recall the storm of

---

[3] *aequor* for both sea and land occurs constantly throughout the *Aeneid.*

book I which harried the forces of Aeneas, even as in the particular
simile at 331–340 the references to Notus and Zephyrus recall those
winds which had earlier been so treacherous and wrathful toward the
Trojans.

The imagistic change of the plain into a sea of battle is elaborated
in the very next simile, also used to describe Turnus:

> ac velut Edoni Boreae cum spiritus alto
> insonat Aegaeo sequiturque ad litora fluctus,
> qua venti incubuere, fugam dant nubila caelo:
> sic Turno, quacumque viam secat, agmina cedunt
> conversaeque ruunt acies; fert impetus ipsum
> et cristam adverso curru quatit aura volantem.
>
> (XII.365–370)

Turnus has become the deadly storm-wind scattering destruction before
him, putting all to flight as he careers in his chariot through the Trojan
lines. In the simile, the storm on the Aegean arises from the effect of the
wind, not from any rain clouds, just as the storm of warfare occurs on
a "clear day," i.e., from a seemingly unprovoked cause, so that Turnus'
attack seems as gratuitous and as irresistible as the wrath of Boreas.

But the similes of storm are not confined to Turnus. For having
recovered from his wound through the intervention of Venus, Aeneas
returns to battle:

> ille volat campoque atrum rapit agmen aperto.
> qualis ubi ad terras abrupto sidere nimbus
> it mare per medium (miseris, heu, praescia longe
> horrescunt corda agricolis: dabit ille ruinas
> arboribus stragemque satis, ruet omnia late),
> ante volant sonitumque ferunt ad litora venti:
> talis in adversos ductor Rhoeteius hostis
> agmen agit, densi cuneis se quisque coactis
> adglomerant.
>
> (XII.450–458)

Aeneas, compared to the rain cloud which heralds the storm, continues in the pattern of the previous two similes. His return presages
the destruction the Latins are soon to experience, even as the rain cloud
presages destruction to the crops of the farmers. The blowing of the
winds bears the noise to the shores, as the heartened cries of Aeneas'
men announce his return. The conflation of the two wind storms comes
clear now, for the battle eventually will be joined between the two

heroes. The language of the storm rising at sea and spreading onto land is used for both and suggests the havoc both are to wreak on their enemies. Their appearance and effect are like natural forces before whose irresistible power all fall. The two heroes conclude the recurrent similes of storms and violent eruptions of nature in these three similes. Between them, ultimately, the issue will be decided, but not before the plain has been stirred up much like a sea. All such language and all such descriptions are meant to recall the opening storm of book I. The terms are reversed, however, for in that scene the forces of nature were, as we saw, personified; here, as they had been from book II on, they form the vehicle for similes used of men. But a further point can also be observed about those storm similes: previously the storms usually were used to describe a body of men, such as the Greeks in book II, or the Trojan youth in book VII, but now the storm similes are used only of two individual men who represent the heart of the storm. The matter has been narrowed to the two essential men who will turn the plain into a massive bloody sea before the defeat of one or the other of them.

A still further observation can be made regarding these similes and their close parallelism to the storm of book I. Aeneas is the active agent in stirring up the violence; he is no longer the passive victim of book I who, when he first appeared in the *Aeneid,* could only hope and pray for the fury to end. Such a transformation has been prepared for in book X where Aeneas was compared to a rainstorm attacking farmer or traveler. But in book XII the promise of that earlier simile is fulfilled as he becomes the instigator of the storm; he has become like the violent wind able to do battle against the might of Turnus, even as Entellus against Dares. The horrible strength of the storm of war which has been growing steadily since book VII now bursts forth in these three similes which locate the source of power in Turnus and Aeneas.

With the emergence of Aeneas, the tide begins to turn against the Latin champion, as the appearance of Juturna in the guise of Metiscus symbolizes. As Juno's agent, Juturna recognizes how perilous is her brother's plight and tries to help. As she drives the chariot, wheeling and darting, she is compared to a black swallow:

> Hoc concussa metu mentem Iuturna virago
> aurigam Turni media inter lora Metiscum
> excutit et longe lapsum temone relinquit;
> ipsa subit manibusque undantis flectit habenas
> cuncta gerens, vocemque et corpus et arma Metisci.
> nigra velut magnas domini cum divitis aedes
> pervolat et pennis alta atria lustrat hirundo

pabula parva legens nidisque loquacibus escas,
et nunc porticibus vacuis, nunc umida circum
stagna sonat: similis medios Iuturna per hostis
fertur equis rapidoque volans obit omnia curru,
iamque hic germanum iamque hic ostentat ovantem
nec conferre manum patitur, volat avia longe.

(XII.468–480)

The description of Juturna's action in lines 468–472 seems an echo of
a simile used of the boat race in book V:

infindunt pariter sulcos, totumque dehiscit
convulsum remis rostrisque tridentibus aequor.
non tam praecipites biiugo certamine campum
corripuere ruuntque effusi carcere currus,
nec sic immissis aurigae undantia lora
concussere iugis pronique in verbera pendent.
tum plausu fremituque virum studiisque faventum
consonat omne nemus, vocemque inclusa volutant
litora, pulsati colles clamore resultant.

(V.142–150)

The boat race was compared to a chariot race, but the passage quoted
indicates that no race on land ever equaled that ship race. In recalling
that passage, the description of Juturna's movements indeed suggests
the final uselessness of her action.

Like the bird, she flits from place to place in her vain attempt to
protect Turnus from his doom. The simile conveys the manner in which
animals, particularly birds, seek to protect their families, but it also
suggests the incoherence and the final uselessness of the birds' endeavor.
Indeed, Juturna will achieve nothing, and even Turnus will turn aside
from her help. Futhermore, Aeneas, like a hunter, is tracking Turnus
at this very moment (XII. 481–487). There can be no salvation, no hope
of escape. Throughout the *Aeneid,* small birds, such as doves, have
appeared in contexts which imply their doom no matter how they
flutter and struggle to escape it. The fact that a black swallow is used
here foretells in the incoherent actions of Juturna the black doom
awaiting Turnus. Like every other agent of Juno, this one, too, will be
defeated, and in her defeat will hasten the end of him she hoped to save.

But not yet does Turnus meet his end. He still possesses considerable potency, and in the next simile he equals Aeneas in terms of power.
Both heroes are waging relentless war on their enemies:

ac velut immissi diversis partibus ignes
arentem in silvam et virgulta sonantia lauro,
aut ubi decursu rapido de montibus altis
dant sonitum spumosi amnes et in aequora currunt
quisque suum populatus iter: non segnius ambo
Aeneas Turnusque ruunt per proelia; nunc, nunc
fluctuat ira intus, rumpuntur nescia vinci
pectora, nunc totis in vulnera viribus itur.

(XII.521–528)

The comparison of the effect of the two men to fire and to a rushing
torrent recalls again the idea that the men are like elemental forces of
nature which sweep away all in their path. Their fierce, sudden, and
desperate attacks are like the effect of fires which seem to spring up
mysteriously in different parts of a forest. The use of fire as a vehicle
for the simile echoes the fire of book II which destroyed Troy, and
which seemed to the fleeing Aeneas like a spontaneously ignited forest
fire. Or again, like Dido's funeral pyre which Aeneas at the beginning
of book V sees but does not comprehend. As on those two former occasions, Aeneas himself is one of the agents of the fire; but the fire is
not the obscure or mysterious destructive force it once was. The simile
recalls, too, the fire of the simile of book X when Pallas as shepherd
started to inflame his men to deeds of daring. The prowess of both
Aeneas and Turnus also ignites the spirits of those around them so that
the fighting like the fire spreads everywhere.

The second member of the simile, the rushing torrent devastating
all it meets, parallels that use of the simile of Aeneas in book X (602–
604), where, embattled, he was compared to a torrent whose effect was
deadly. The power of the simile derives its strength ultimately from the
simile used of the Greeks in book II (494–499) who burst into Priam's
chamber like a river bursting its dam. The river became a river of death
for the royal family of Troy, and so here the torrent too is one of
death. The deliberate recalling, by the simile, of Troy's destruction
focuses attention on the fact that this conflict between Trojan and
Latin is a variation of the theme of the fall of Troy. But certain
changes have occurred which distinguish this battle from the earlier
one. The Trojans are not like the invading Greeks, for their mission is
not to destroy civilization but to found it; the people invaded, insofar
as they follow the cause of Turnus, are trying to withstand the advent
of civilization and of the future. But defeat alone awaits them. Moreover, the simile reminds us, too, of the baneful destructive fire which

was that of Troy. By its recollection of the past, the simile points out how thin a difference distinguishes the good and the bad in warfare, and how dire war is. The point can be observed in the simile's yoking together the incompatible fire and water, just as Aeneas and Turnus are yoked together in their deadly pursuits. Whether Aeneas is water and Turnus fire, death by fire or water is still death.

One further point deserves comment. In this simile of book XII, Aeneas has taken on the role of avenger, albeit reluctantly, for it was not his intention to engage the Latin host for its destruction; the breaking of the truce forced him to fight. But in doing so he fulfills at last the desire he had for defending his ancient homeland of Troy. There he was unsuccessful and forbidden to fight on behalf of Troy. Now he does fight, and fights, as the episodes show, in full awareness of what it means to battle. The wish of book II is fulfilled in book XII, and the cost of realizing that wish is enormous.

The effect of the fighting begins to tell on the Latins, especially those within the walled city. Confusion breaks out with some advocating one thing, others, another. Their behavior is compared to a swarm of bees who are being smoked out from a sheltering rock:

> exoritur trepidos inter discordia civis:
> urbem alii reserare iubent et pandere portas
> Dardanidis ipsumque trahunt in moenia regem;
> arma ferunt alii et pergunt defendere muros,
> inclusas ut cum latebroso in pumice pastor
> vest'gavit apes fumoque implevit amaro;
> illae intus trepidae rerum per cerea castra
> discurrunt magnisque acuunt stridoribus iras;
> volvitur ater odor tectis, tum murmure caeco
> intus saxa sonant, vacuas it fumus ad auras.
> (XII.583–592)

The simile accurately captures the confusion within the city besieged by the Trojans. It recalls the incident described in book VII when a sudden swarm of bees within Latinus' palace was held to portend the coming of the stranger who would eventually reign in the citadel (VII. 59–67). Indeed, the simile not only recalls this incident but shows the fulfillment of the prophecy.[4] It is difficult not to see here also a designed variation on the bee simile connected with the building of Carthage. Whereas the Carthaginian bees were members of a hive, that is to say,

---

[4] Observe that the bees settle in a sacred laurel in Latinus' palace, a fact which recalls the laurel in the heart of Priam's palace (II. 513).

of an ordered society working together for the common good and for more than their own community since they produced honey for men, the Latin bees are merely a swarm. This swarm has not built its own home but has found the chance refuge offered by a honeycombed rock. The swarm apparently produces nothing, certainly nothing beyond its own needs; though it is harmless in itself so long as it is not disturbed, it becomes a threat to any different kind of society and is itself threatened by any outside force. Thus, the shepherd finding the swarm where his flocks are to feed must smoke it out for their protection. The bee similes of Carthage (I. 430 ff.) and of the Latins sum up totally different views of the human community held by Aeneas and the Latins, their inevitable conflict, and their necessary destruction of one by the other. The point has been prepared for by the description Latinus has given of Latin society under his rule, which is a veritable golden age (VII. 202–204). But the golden age of Latinus is coming to an end, for he has no son to whom he can transfer his inheritance. Furthermore, his people are assailed by such outsiders as Turnus and Mezentius. The Latins like the swarm of bees in the simile of book XII can live in peace only so long as they are not disturbed by an external force. The golden age of Latinus cannot survive and must be replaced by a new social order. The leader of that social order needs to be one who understands that the ideal aim of a human community is to reflect, in so far as possible, the harmony of the universe. Such a leader is, of course, Aeneas who, in his encounter with Anchises in the Elysian fields, first heard the dulcet murmuring of the harmonious souls as bees buzzing in a glade and learned there what civilization meant (VI. 707 ff.).

But in order to bring civilization to pass, the hostile leader Turnus must be brought low. He himself helps the process, for having admitted that he recognizes the disguised Juturna and feeling the reproaches of Saces, whose speech is not unlike the bitter remarks of Drances in book XI (124–131), Turnus elects to return to his original vow of single combat with Aeneas. He deserts his sister, and rushes through his enemy's weapons to find the Trojan leader. His course is described in a simile:

> ac veluti montis saxum de vertice praeceps
> cum ruit avulsum vento, seu turbidus imber
> proluit aut annis solvit sublapsa vetustas;
> fertur in abruptum magno mons improbus actu
> exsultatque solo, silvas armenta virosque
> involvens secum: disiecta per agmina Turnus
> sic urbis ruit ad muros, ubi plurima fuso

sanguine terra madet striduntque hastilibus aurae,
significatque manu et magno simul incipit ore:
(XII.684–692)

Turnus' movement is like a loosened rock rolling down a mountainside; he, like the rock, rushes headlong to his fate. The reproaches of Saces recall Drances' reproaches and effectively shake him so that he no longer can withstand the sense of shame his recent behavior has caused him. The reproaches affect Turnus just as a rock is loosened by the action of the elements. Once started on his path Turnus moves by his own inertia sweeping all before him. The simile continues the pattern of natural phenomena already evident in the book and suggests again the mindlessness of the phenomena.

The simile forms a dramatic contrast to his previous circular motions in the chariot driven by Juturna. Those twistings and turnings were the visible signs of his inner turmoil, of the indecision of his mind which for long had wavered; now there are to be no more evasions for Turnus; he moves in one straight line. The episode of Turnus' return follows upon the narration of Amata's death. Amata, by hanging herself because she feared that Turnus, so long absent from the battle, had died, brings to an end a series of mad acts which began when she was bitten by the serpent of Allecto. The serpent, by entwining itself within the very core of Amata, spread its venom and caused her destructive behavior, like that of a bacchante. As the poison started to work she was compared to a top set in motion by young boys:

ceu quondam torto volitans sub verbere turbo,
quem pueri magno in gyro vacua atria circum
intenti ludo exercent—ille actus habena
curvatis fertur spatiis; stupet inscia supra
impubesque manus mirata volubile buxum;
dant animos plagae: non cursu segnior illo
per medias urbes agitur populosque ferocis.
(VII.378–384)

Amata became like the inanimate object whose movement is controlled from outside. The goads of the serpent and its poison are like the whips which lash the top into movement; she is driven to wandering through the city in a frenzy, just as once before Dido, driven by the wound of love, wandered like a bacchante. The frenzied behavior of Amata finally spends itself in her last violent act of suicide.

But Amata is closely connected with Turnus. Both are inflamed by

Allecto, both commit outrageous acts which ensure the war's taking place. Furthermore, Amata's relationship to Turnus has been dubious: does she really want him only as a son-in-law? Then, too, her death immediately precedes Turnus' resolute acceptance of the armed combat with Aeneas and thereby anticipates Turnus' own death. Finally, there is a close parallel between Amata's whirling like a top throughout the city and the wide circles Turnus' own chariot makes on the battlefield. In being driven by Juturna, he too has been like an object set in motion by an outside force. He has become, in other words, the spinning top which once was used to describe Amata. In those widening circles, he repeats the pattern Amata had begun. With her death by hanging, he, too, ceases to wander and rolls like a boulder headlong and heedless to his final doom. Closely connected as Amata and Turnus have been, they are never more so than in the final episodes of their lives.

Aeneas, upon hearing of Turnus' return to the combat, leaves his siege of the walls and citadel and goes forth to meet his enemy. His approach is described in what seems at first glance to be an odd simile:

> At pater Aeneas audito nomine Turni
> deserit et muros et summas deserit arces
> praecipitatque moras omnis, opera omnia rumpit
> laetitia exsultans horrendumque intonat armis:
> quantus Athos aut quantus Eryx aut ipse coruscis
> cum fremit ilicibus quantus gaudetque nivali
> vertice se attollens pater Appenninus ad auras.
> (XII.697–703)

The comparison of Aeneas rushing to meet his foe to three tall mountains seems almost inappropriate. The only point of obvious comparison lies between his clashing arms and the tossing ilexes on the Apennines (and by implication on Athos and Mt. Eryx). But, upon reflection, we find that the simile becomes more and more appropriate, for what Vergil is describing is the mighty appearance of Aeneas whose valor and strength, as well as his determination, raise him above all other men (XII. 704–707). He has become like those mountains which command men's eyes to gaze upon them because they dwarf all else around them. What Vergil compares here is the quality of the man to the quality of the mass of mountain. Significantly, this is the first occasion in the *Aeneid* when Aeneas himself has been compared to a rocky cliff or a mountain. Both Latinus and Mezentius had been earlier described as such, and now Aeneas outdistances them; even Latinus is amazed. Aeneas has become a figure of strength, immovable, unyielding, towering over everyone else, and far transcending the fragile creature who first appeared in book I. In this new capacity, he towers just as Neptune towered over the raging seas. The comparison is not farfetched when we recall that the plain has become in metaphor a sea of battle where the tides of men are washed back and forth. As Neptune, described in the simile of the statesman, calmed the stormy sea, so here Aeneas, who repeatedly throughout book XII has tried to act the role of statesman, especially in calming the passions roused on both sides by the breaking of the truce, now at last realizes his goal; the battle between Latins and Trojans ceases as he approaches, and the conflict wherein Aeneas will prove that he is the victorious warrior now centers on the two heroes.

The effect on the people of the coming together of Aeneas and Turnus is immediate and is described in a complex simile:

> ac velut ingenti Sila summove Taburno
> cum duo conversis inimica in proelia tauri
> frontibus incurrunt, pavidi cessere magistri,
> stat pecus omne metu mutum, mussantque iuvencae
> quis nemori imperitet, quem tota armenta sequantur;
> illi inter sese multa vi vulnera miscent
> cornuaque obnixi infigunt et sanguine largo
> colla armosque lavant, gemitu nemus omne remugit:
> non aliter Tros Aeneas et Daunius heros
> concurrunt clipeis, ingens fragor aethera complet.
>
> (XII.715–724)

The two leaders are comparable to the bulls engaging in battle, and their people to the frightened herds standing by, awaiting the outcome of the bloody conflict to show which leader they will follow. By comparing Aeneas and Turnus to battling bulls, the simile recalls the earlier one of book XII which compared Turnus, about to go off to engage in single combat, to a bull preparing for the attack. Here, then, is the fulfillment of that earlier simile. But the simile's details in their description of the inflicted wounds and the struggling of great forces advances the very action itself. But it is not only the leaders who in their conflict are like the animals, so also are the people, for they become like herds, lowing and fearful. However, the simile contains a further implication, for the herds, as a result of the conflict of the leaders, are to be merged into one herd, no matter what the outcome. Thus, the simile anticipates the final goal for which Aeneas since book VII has been struggling: the merging of Latins and Trojans.

This simile like the others which draw on the animal world to describe the behavior of men appears natural enough in its illumination of the ferocity of the men. Although it has the advantage of singling out one idea, that of ferocity, to concentrate on, the simile nevertheless reduces men, whose motives are complex, to the level of creatures instinctively responding to what threatens them. Even Aeneas becomes enveloped in this reduction for the first time since book II. The behavior of the men, their very actions, of course, are what cause the similes to be felt as appropriate. But, furthermore, the fact that Aeneas is again so involved sheds light on this particular episode. Aeneas has no choice but to fight on Turnus' terms. Turnus' *violentia* has reduced not only himself but his enemy and all the people around him to the level of beasts. Insofar as all are reduced, by so much are they culpable for acting less than human. Aeneas does not want the deadly slaughter which Turnus has caused for the Trojans and Latins as well as for himself, but no way out exists, and it is in such a closed world, where the alternatives are so sharply delineated, that mortal affairs acquire their most tragic tone.

In the course of the conflict Turnus strikes with his sword only to have it shatter like ice:

> . . . postquam arma dei ad Volcania ventum est,
> mortalis mucro glacies ceu futtilis ictu
> dissiluit, fulva resplendent fragmina harena.
> (XII.739–741)

The sword had served well enough in the course of the battle so long as it did not have to come against the arms of Vulcan, but against the divine arms it is powerless; just as ice it leaps apart. The simile is a slight one and, indeed, it is the only simile of ice in the entire *Aeneid*; nevertheless it is not simply ornamental. First of all, the shattering of the sword hastens the end of Turnus. His weapons are as useless as would be those made of ice against Aeneas. But furthermore, the fact that in his rush to engage in battle he left his own sword behind and snatched at that of Metiscus reveals how improvident, how thoughtless of himself Turnus has been. Such disregard of weapons is hardly the mark of a first-class warrior; Turnus is less than the best, and despite his initial success with the sword, at the crucial point it failed him, even as ice no matter how sharp initially it might be will ultimately shatter or melt in the presence of heat. In this headlong recklessness, Turnus gives evidence of being less than the man he supposes himself to be and more like the animal of the repeated similes. His very actions, even with regard to himself, support the contention that his *violentia* had reduced him to the level of the beasts.

The very next simile continues the point, for in it Turnus in his panic flight is compared to a stag pursued by a hunting dog:

> Nec minus Aeneas, quamquam tardata sagitta
> interdum genua impediunt cursumque recusant,
> insequitur trepidique pedem pede fervidus urget:
> inclusum veluti si quando flumine nactus
> cervum aut puniceae saeptum formidine pennae
> venator cursu canis et latratibus instat;
> ille autem insidiis et ripa territus alta
> mille fugit refugitque vias, at vividus Vmber
> haeret hians, iam iamque tenet similisque tenenti
> increpuit malis morsuque elusus inani est;
> tum vero exoritur clamor ripaeque lacusque
> responsant circa et caelum tonat omne tumultu.
>
> (XII.746–757)

This final simile drawn from the animal world reveals Turnus as the stag pursued almost to its death. He has become the frightened animal whose only hope is to outrun the dog. Again the simile advances the action at the same time it defines it. For Turnus there will be no hope of escape. The simile iterates the original cause for the war between Trojans and Latins, Silvia's deer inadvertently killed by the dogs of Ascanius. Turnus, the chief antagonist to the Trojans, unlike the doe of Dido's simile (IV. 68–73), becomes the stag which learns at last the panic of fear. All the might and strength of the animal similes which had been used earlier of Turnus are reduced to the picture of the hunted stag. There remains for Turnus only this final reduction in the animal similes. What had been implicit in all of them, namely the inherent inferiority of the animal, and therefore its vulnerability, has at last been proved. Because of Turnus' frightened flight, Aeneas is forced into pursuit. Though Turnus' behavior is natural enough, it nonetheless reveals again how far he is from his conception of the hero willing to advance nobly to the fray. By forcing Aeneas to pursue him, he again forces Aeneas to fight on his terms, terms which gain him only a little time. In the simile, Aeneas is again reduced to an animal, just as Turnus is; he becomes like a hunting dog. The simile repeats the idea seen earlier in the simile of the two bulls. By arranging his simile in this fashion Vergil elicits pity for the pursued Turnus, but it is a controlled pity, for the language of the simile with its medley of human and canine imagery in lines 751 ff. creates an ambiguity about the hunting dog.[5]

In order to conclude the action of the gods and to create suspense, Vergil here interrupts his narrative to tell of the reconciliation of Juno to the will of Jupiter. The first consequence of that reconciliation is Jupiter's sending a Fury to warn Juturna to cease from her attempts to help the helpless Turnus. The approach of the Fury is compared to the flight of an arrow tipped with venom thrown by a Parthian or a Cydonian:

> non secus ac nervo per nubem impulsa sagitta,
> armatam saevi Parthus quam felle veneni,
> Parthus sive Cydon, telum immedicabile, torsit,
> stridens et celeris incognita transilit umbras:
> talis se sata Nocte tulit terrasque petivit.
>
> (XII.856–860)

The simile captures not only the swiftness of the Fury's flight but its deadly mission as well, for like the poisoned arrow it will inflict on Juturna a wound of grief that will never heal since it is the harbinger of Turnus' doom. In this it is like the *letalis harundo* of the shepherd in the doe simile of Dido (IV. 73). The fact that an arrow is used to describe the flight recalls also the arrow Acestes shot (V. 519–540). There the arrow had burst into flame like a meteor and had been regarded as a good omen by Aeneas and the Trojans; again the arrow becomes an omen of good for Aeneas. Furthermore, since the Fury is sent from Hades and is a daughter of Night, she is related to the Fury Allecto who as agent of Juno caused such mischief in book VII. Fittingly, the same source which supplied the occasion for the outbreak of the war should supply the herald of its ending. The fact that it is a Parthian arrow underscores this point, for Juturna, an immortal, did not expect another immortal to behave so treacherously. Finally, too, the fact that the Fury moves to earth in a whirlwind, putting an end to

---

[5] Although commentators and Lewis and Short take *canis* as nominative in apposition to *venator*, it need not be so construed. *Canis* could be genitive, as Mackail translates (*Vergil's Works,* p. 256), but in his commentary, *ad loc,* he interprets the phrase as "hunting dog." The support of the usual interpretation seems to come from the use of *morsuque elusus inani est,* but the phrase seems ambiguous. Does it really need to apply to the dog? To cite *Vmber* in 753 is no help, though Lewis and Short supply *canis* there; nor is *hians,* a term applicable to human beings as well as dogs. I have construed the passage in the usual fashion, and hesitantly have based my remarks on that interpretation. For a different interpretation of this simile see Putnam, pp. 187 ff.

the whirling of the hunted Turnus, resolves at last the storm imagery of the *Aeneid*. The poisoned Parthian arrow whirring to earth and twisting unobserved through the shadows neatly embraces all these connotations. Juturna feels its effect immediately, and in her lamentation for Turnus she forbodes his impending destruction.

But Turnus attempts once more to rescue himself. He tries to hurl a stone at Aeneas but his attempt fails. His efforts are compared to those of a man struggling in a nightmare:

> ac velut in somnis, oculos ubi languida pressit
> nocte quies, nequiquam avidos extendere cursus
> velle videmur et in mediis conatibus aegri
> succidimus; non lingua valet, non corpore notae
> sufficiunt vires nec vox aut verba sequuntur:
> sic Turno, quacumque viam virtute petivit,
> successum dea dira negat.
>
> (XII.908–914)

Turnus' failure to win his goal with the stone becomes symbolic of his failure to act successfully. The dread goddess—the Fury, specifically—denies his success. The sense of frustration Turnus feels is conveyed by the simile which draws on the experience familiar to most men of trying to run in a dream but unable to do so, of weakness overwhelming any attempt at movement, of the failure of both speech and words. Not only do the physical resources of the man in the grip of a nightmare fail him, but so does his ability to call for help or to explain his failure to himself. His frustration leaves him utterly powerless.

Turnus acts like a man who dreams. As the final simile used of Turnus in the *Aeneid,* it comments not only on his present failure but also on his entire career in the struggle between Trojan and Latin. He has always been a man in a dream, for what he has pursued and what he has hoped for from the very beginning were illusory goals which could only lead him to frustration and defeat. The point was vividly made in an earlier simile in book X, a simile whose implications are realized only at the end of book XII. In book X, in order to rescue Turnus from what might well have been his destruction at the hands of Aeneas, angry at the death of Pallas, Juno fashioned a hollow cloud in the shape of the Trojan leader so that Turnus might be lured away. The ruse works, and Turnus is beguiled to board a ship which takes him to his fatherland. The simile to describe this apparition compares it to the shapes which flit at the time of death or which delude the sleeping senses:

tum dea nube cava tenuem sine viribus umbram
in faciem Aeneae (visu mirabile monstrum)
Dardaniis ornat telis, clipeumque iubasque
divini adsimulat capitis, dat inania verba,
dat sine mente sonum gressusque effingit euntis,
morte obita qualis fama est volitare figuras
aut quae sopitos deludunt somnia sensus.

(X.636–642)

The *imago* Juno devises is eminently successful, yet it is so because
Turnus himself is willing to be misled. Thinking that he wants to
prove his power against Aeneas, he runs after what looks like him. But
in the light of the final encounter between the two leaders in book
XII, an encounter long postponed by Turnus, it becomes evident that
Turnus did not, and probably never did want to meet his enemy. The
frenzied motions he goes through to escape Aeneas, even at the very
end, suggest that the reality of confronting Aeneas was more than he
could bear. The realization of the trick played upon him by the goddess in book X causes him anguish, for he sees for a moment his own
evasion of his responsibility; through a flash of insight engendered by
his fears for his public reputation, Turnus bears witness to his failure.
Yet his every action from book VII onwards has been futile and powerless, like that of a man in a dream, for Turnus is incapable of long
sustaining the sight of reality. This point Vergil has made abundantly
clear to his audience in Turnus' actions in books IX–XII. But he has
also made it evident in the first appearance of Turnus in book VII.
For Turnus in sleep is confronted by Allecto, and his arrogant boast
(VII. 435 ff.) so angers that Fury that she casts her venomous serpent
on him, thereby confirming him in his violent madness. From his mad
dream of glory Turnus never awakes. The simile of the dream fittingly describes not only Turnus' action in that book, but his actions
throughout the *Aeneid*. He has been living in the nightmare world of
unreality, a world in which only his personal fame is of concern to
him; from the start he has been deluded. This last simile defines and
characterizes Turnus, and the *coup de grace* is the detail of the dread
goddess preventing his success. The *dira dea* embraces not only the
Fury sent by Jupiter, but Allecto, and also the goddess Juno in whose
care he had originally placed himself. But the dread goddess is also his
own vanity which forever prevented him from perceiving the reality
of Aeneas and the condition of his own life. Turnus ironically founders on the public reputation of his own strength. The reality utterly
splinters him.

The dream-like delusion of Turnus is comparable to the deluded world Dido lives in. Both figures are parallel in their refusal and consequent inability to see anything other than what they want to. Both are preoccupied with their own fame, their reputation—note how Turnus, aware of his lack of strength, turns his eyes upon those surrounding him, as though seeking some sign of reassurance (XII. 914–918)—the most obvious form of delusion. By way of contrast, Aeneas is not concerned over his reputation, for, as he tells Ascanius, he wants to show forth *virtus* and *verus labor* (XII. 435). Both Dido and Turnus founder on the reality Aeneas himself both represents and is. This becomes evident in language Vergil uses to describe Aeneas' successful hurling of his spear against Turnus:

> Cunctanti telum Aeneas fatale coruscat,
> sortitus fortunam oculis, et corpore toto
> eminus intorquet. murali concita numquam
> tormento sic saxa fremunt nec fulmine tanti
> dissultant crepitus. volat atri turbinis instar
> exitium dirum hasta ferens orasque recludit
> loricae et clipei extremos septemplicis orbis;
> per medium stridens transit femur. incidit ictus
> ingens ad terram duplicato poplite Turnus.
> (XII.919–927)

Patiently, Aeneas has tracked his enemy and waited for the opportune moment. He is rewarded by his success in bringing Turnus down. In describing the weapon's course, moreover, Vergil achieves a subtlety of characterization which derives from Homer and transcends his effort.[6] The weapon becomes in Vergil's language an instrument of divine will as well as one of human agency. To compare it to the thunderbolt is tantamount to comparing its hurler to the god who wields the lightning, Jupiter. Aeneas, in bringing low Turnus, acts as the human agent for the divine purpose. As the description of the trajectory of the spear continues, it becomes evident that the weapon itself, the instrument of death, is like the whirlwind which once stirred up the sea. Again Aeneas is the author of this storm. He perfectly realizes in his act his role as creator of storms.

But the final witness of Aeneas' completeness as heroic statesman and bearer of civilization occurs only when Aeneas finally slays Turnus. The confrontation between them is worth more than a passing

---

[6] Homer, *Iliad*, 7. 263–272.

glance. Aeneas' spear pierces Turnus below the thigh and he falls. He speaks thus to Aene? ·

> ille humilis supplexque oculos dextramque precantem
> protendens 'equidem merui nec deprecor' inquit;
> 'utere sorte tua. miseri te si qua parentis
> tangere cura potest, oro (fuit et tibi talis
> Anchises genitor) Dauni miserere senectae
> et me, seu corpus spoliatum lumine mavis,
> redde meis. vicisti et victum tendere palmas
> Ausonii videre; tua est Lavinia coniunx,
> ulterius ne tende odiis.'
>
> (XII.930–938)

Turnus admits that he deserves to be conquered and even to die. At the same time he pleads for compassion for his aged father, and on those grounds begs Aeneas to spare his, Turnus', life, or if this may not be, to return his dead body to his father. He further suggests that since he is vanquished and that Lavinia will be Aeneas' in marriage, the Trojan has nothing more to gain by pressing hatred further.

Both by his words and by his gestures, as Vergil describes them, Turnus is begging for his life as no other hero in the *Aeneid* has deigned to do, and this despite his claim that he is not asking for mercy. In his appeal to Aeneas, he invokes filial piety and parental love, feelings which he himself not only disdained but outraged on the occasion of Pallas' death.[7] Turnus' behavior and speech when he is vanquished suggest one of two things, either that Turnus has an incredible capacity for self-delusion, for not seeing the contradictions, the dichotomies, in his behavior and words, or that he is profoundly hypocritical. His speech to Aeneas is full of equivocation; it is a cloak of nobility, courage, and piety concealing the reality of Turnus; it is meant to deceive or to seduce Aeneas into error. And it almost does, for the appeal to filial piety is a strong one for Aeneas. But to succumb to Turnus' plea would have made a mockery of Pallas' death and of Aeneas' pledge to Euander. But Aeneas suddenly realizes that the armor Turnus is wearing is that of the slain Pallas, and the true nature of Turnus' "heroism" is abruptly revealed to him.[8] He sees through the coruscating cloak of words to the ugly truth beneath, and

---

[7] X. 441–443 and 491–495. Note how in this latter speech Turnus echoes Pyrrhus' words to Priam, II. 547–550.

[8] For a discussion of Turnus with the arms of Pallas, see my article in *P. Q.*, 357–359.

he kills Turnus, in recognition of the fact that such men have no place in the new world.

The slaying of Turnus is in a sense Aeneas' first and necessary act of statesmanship, in which is made manifest the function of his moral education and his awareness of responsibility: for what must be eradicated if the new civilized world is to come to pass is the ethos which holds that, as in the animal world, might makes right, that men live by preying on men, and that speech which most distinguishes man from beast is an instrument not of truth but of power, a weapon against other men. In killing Turnus, Aeneas sacrifices him to Pallas and Euander and demonstrates thereby his *humanitas* and his *pietas* and so proclaims his own sense of responsibility. Thus Turnus, in his death, fulfills the role of sacrificial animal that his *violentia* had for so long promised.

Book XII is a book of endings and conclusions. As the narrative reaches its climax so also do the patterns of the similes. The threads deployed so carefully throughout the *Aeneid* are here drawn together to complete the design. The animal similes of book XII conclude the pattern of similes in the rest of the epic with the sacrifice of the man who in his blindness would reduce all men to the level of animals. The storm with which the *Aeneid* opens finds its counterpart in the battlefield of book XII wherein the hero once its victim becomes the author of the storm. The destructive power of natural forces is finally laid to rest in book XII, and the man who once was tempest tossed becomes the mountain of strength. The world of illusion founders at last on the rock of reality. The bearer of civilization at last ensures that the city he was destined to found can be born.

Throughout the last book, Vergil's epic hero does not have the lion's share of the similes. Indeed, remarkably few are devoted to him, even as relatively few have been devoted to him throughout the *Aeneid*.[9] Very likely the reason for this is that Aeneas' actions are self-defining and in general need little of the explanatory or characterizing qualities that the Vergilian simile exhibits. Vergil's self-conscious and civilized hero's actions mirror his inward being, in contrast with Dido or Turnus whose divided souls are constantly reflected in the similes which imply as well the consequences of that dichotomy. In book XII we witness the hero as whole man, who dominates and concludes the action.

---

[9] In only 14 of the 116 similes does Aeneas have a part, as compared to the 19 in which Turnus appears.

# Latin Passages
# Cited in the Text

Similes are indicated by *italics*.
Numbers after the colon refer to pages in this book.

# Bibliography of Useful Works
# and Works Cited in Text

## BOOKS

Austin, R. G., ed. *Virgil Aeneid II*. Oxford: Clarendon Press, 1964.

————, ed. *Virgil Aeneid IV*. Oxford: Clarendon Press, 1955.

Büchner, K. "P. Vergilius Maro, der Dichter der Römer," in Pauly-Wissowa, *Realencyclopädie der Classischen Altertumswissenschaft*, Band VIII A 1–2, cols. 1021–1486 (on the *Aeneid* cols. 1337–1486). Published separately as *P. Vergilius Maro, der Dichter der Römer*. Stuttgart: Alfred Druckenmuller Verlag, 1956.

Constans, L. A. *L'Énéide de Virgile, étude et analyse*. Paris: Mallotie, 1938.

Conway, R. S. *Harvard Lectures on the Vergilian Age*. Cambridge: Harvard University Press, 1928.

Duckworth, G. E. *Structural Patterns and Proportions in Vergil's Aeneid*. Ann Arbor: University of Michigan Press, 1962.

Fletcher, Frank, ed. *Virgil Aeneid VI*. Oxford: Clarendon Press, 1941. Reprinted with corrections 1962.

Guillemin, A. M. *L'Originalité de Vergile*. Paris: Les Belles Lettres, 1931.

————. *Vergile: poète, artiste, et penseur*. Paris: Michel, 1951.

Hirtzel, F. A., ed. *P. Vergili Maronis Opera*. Oxford: Clarendon Press, 1900.

Heinze, R. *Virgils Epische Technik*. 4th ed. Leipzig: B. G. Teubner, 1903; 4th ed., 1928.

Knauer, G. N. *Die Aeneis und Homer; Studien zur poetischen Technik Vergils mit Listen der Homerzitate in der Aeneis* (*Hypomnemata* Heft 7). Göttingen: Vandenhoeck und Ruprecht, 1964.

Knight, W. F. J. *Roman Vergil*. London: Faber and Faber, 1944; 2nd ed., 1946.

————. *Accentual Symmetry in Vergil*. Oxford: B. Blackwell, 1939.

Lattimore, R., trans. *The Iliad of Homer*. Chicago: University of Chicago Press, 1951.

Mackail, J. W., ed. *The Aeneid*. Oxford: Clarendon Press, 1930.

————, trans. *Virgil's Works*. New York: The Modern Library, 1934.

Mynors, R. A. B., ed. *P. Vergili Maronis Opera*. Oxford: Clarendon Press, 1969.

Norden, E. *P. Vergilius Maro Aeneis Buch VI*. Leipzig: B. G. Teubner, 1903; 2nd ed., 1916.

Nowottny, Winifred. *The Language Poets Use*. London: Althone Press, 1962.

Otis, Brooks. *Virgil: A Study in Civilized Poetry*. Oxford: Clarendon Press, 1963.

Paratore, E. *Virgilio*. Roma: Faro, 1945; 2nd ed., Firenze, 1954.

Perret, J. *Virgile, l'homme et l'oeuvre*. Paris: Boivin, 1952.

Pöschl, Viktor. *Die Dichtkunst Virgils: Bild und Symbol in der Äneis*. Innsbruck: M. F. Rohrer, 1950. Trans. by Gerda Seligson as *The Art of Vergil: Image and Symbol in the Aeneid*. Ann Arbor: University of Michigan Press, 1962.

Prescott, H. W. *The Development of Virgil's Art*. Chicago: University of Chicago Press, 1927.

Putnam, M. C. J. *The Poetry of the Aeneid*. Cambridge: Harvard University Press, 1965.

Quinn, K. *Latin Explorations: Critical Studies in Roman Literature*. London: Routledge and Kegan Paul, 1963.

_____. *Virgil's Aeneid: A Critical Description*. London: Routledge and Kegan Paul, 1968.

Schmitz, A. *Infelix Dido: Étude esthétique et psychologique du livre IV de l'Énéide de Virgile*. Gembloux, Belgium: J. Duculot, S.A., 1960.

*Servianorum in Vergilii Carmina Commentariorum*. Editio Harvardiana, vols. II and III, Special Publications of The American Philological Association, Lancaster, Pa., 1946; 1965.

*Servii Grammatici qui feruntur in Vergilii Carmina Commentarii*, eds. G. Thilo et H. Hagen. 2 vols. Leipzig: B. G. Teubner, 1884.

Shewan, A. *Homeric Essays*. Oxford: B. Blackwell, 1935.

Stanford, W. Bedell. *Greek Metaphor: Studies in Theory and Practice*. Oxford: B. Blackwell, 1936.

Wace, A. J. B. and Stubbings, F. H. *A Companion to Homer*. London: Macmillan and Co., 1962.

Wetmore, M. N. *Index Verborum Vergilianus*. Hildesheim: Georg Olms, 1961. (A reprint of the 1930 Yale University Press edition.)

Williams, R. D., ed. *Virgil Aeneid III*. Oxford: Clarendon Press, 1962.

_____, ed. *Virgil Aeneid V*. Oxford: Clarendon Press, 1960.

# ARTICLES

Anderson, W. D. "Notes on the Simile in Homer and His Successors: I. Homer, Apollonius Rhodius, and Vergil," *Classical Journal* LIII (1957), 81–87.

Brooks, R. "*Discolor Aura*. Reflections on the Golden Bough," *American Journal of Philology* LXXIV (1953), 260–280.

Coffey, M. "The Subject Matter of Vergil's Similes," *Bulletin of the Institute of Classical Studies of the University of London* VIII (1961), 63–75.

Covi, Madeline C. "Dido in Vergil's *Aeneid*," *Classical Journal* LX (1964), 57–60.

Dahlmann, H. "Der Bienenstaat in Vergils Georgika," *Akad. der wiss. Mainz, abhand. Geistes und Sozialwiss. Klass.* 10 (1954).

Dolzani, C. "Valori drammatici ed elementi chiaroscurali del II libro dell' Eneide," *Atene e Roma* IX (1941), 177–179.

Duckworth, G. E. "The Architecture of the *Aeneid*," *American Journal of Philology* LXXV (1954), 1–15.

_____. "The *Aeneid* as a Trilogy," *Transactions of the American Philological Association* LXXXVIII (1957), 1–10.

_____. "Recent Work on Vergil: A Bibliographical Survey 1940–1956," *Classical World* LI (1958), 89–92, 116–117, 123–128, 151–159, 185–193, 228–235. Reprinted separately by the Vergilian Society Inc., 1964.

_____. "Tripartite Structure in the *Aeneid*," *Vergilius* VII (1961), 2–11.

_____. "Recent Work on Vergil: A Bibliographical Survey 1957–1963," *Classical World* LVII (1963–1964), 193–228. Reprinted by the Vergilian Society, 1964.

Fenik, B. "Parallelism of Theme and Imagery in *Aeneid* II and IV," *American Journal of Philology* LXXX (1959), 1–24.

Fränkel, E. "Some Aspects of the Structure of *Aeneid* VII," *Journal of Roman Studies* XXXV (1945), 1–14.

Hornsby, R. A. "The Vergilian Simile as Means of Judgment," *Classical Journal* LX (1965), 337–341.

_____. "The Armor of the Slain," *Philological Quarterly* XLV (1966), 347–359.

Howe, T. P. "Color Imagery in *Macbeth* I and II and the *Aeneid* II: A Pedagogic Experiment," *Classical Journal* LI (1955), 322–327.

Knox, B. M. W. "The Serpent and the Flame: The Imagery of the Second Book of the *Aeneid*," *American Journal of Philology,* LXXI (1950), 379–400.

Newton, Francis. "Recurrent Imagery in *Aeneid* IV," *Transactions of the American Philological Association* LXXXVIII (1957), 31–43.

von Duhn, M. "Die Gleichnisse in den Allectoszenen des 7 Buches von Vergils *Aeneis*," *Gymnasium* LXIV (1957), 59–83.

# Index